Flying the Dream, On

This Ferry Pilot
Doesn't
Look Down

SANFORD *and* DIANE REIM

This Ferry Pilot Doesn't Look Down
Flying the Dream, One Airplane at a Time
All Rights Reserved.
Copyright © 2022 Sanford and Diane Reim
v2.0

The opinions expressed in this manuscript are solely the opinions of the author and do not represent the opinions or thoughts of the publisher. The author has represented and warranted full ownership and/or legal right to publish all the materials in this book.

This book may not be reproduced, transmitted, or stored in whole or in part by any means, including graphic, electronic, or mechanical without the express written consent of the publisher except in the case of brief quotations embodied in critical articles and reviews.

Outskirts Press, Inc.
http://www.outskirtspress.com

ISBN: 978-1-9772-5179-4

Cover Photo © 2022 Sanford and Diane Reim. All rights reserved - used with permission.

Outskirts Press and the "OP" logo are trademarks belonging to Outskirts Press, Inc.

PRINTED IN THE UNITED STATES OF AMERICA

TABLE OF CONTENTS

Foreword and Dedication	i
Chapter 1: Super Breezy – Times Two	1
Chapter 2: The Introduction	15
Chapter 3: Bush-Wacking	20
Chapter 4: First Fly-In Fishing Trip	23
Chapter 5: Finding the Floats	28
Chapter 6: Thanks, but No Thanks!	35
Chapter 7: Oatmeal and Lake Water	39
Chapter 8: Rainy Lake Rescues	45
Chapter 9: The Last Frontier	56
Chapter 10: Marv's Journey	68
Chapter 11: The Inside Passage to the Last Frontier	76
Chapter 12: Dreaming to Fly – Flying the Dream	80
Chapter 13: Taking the Southern Route	88

Chapter 14: The Engine Just Did What?	94
Chapter 15: Delivery Service	100
Chapter 16: Wearing the Airplane	117
Chapter 17: Every Airplane has a Story	121
Chapter 18: School of Hard Knocks	125
Chapter 19: Chasing the Breezy	130
Chapter 20: Chasing the Breezy – After the Show	144
Chapter 21: Where there's Smoke, there's Fire…and a Raven	148
Chapter 22: Bandits on the Run	160
Chapter 23: Red-Neck Flying	166
Chapter 24: Surprise, Surprise	174
Chapter 25: Our Guardian Angels	179

Foreword and Dedication

We had no idea where the adventures were…we just let the airplane take us there.

Sanford and I have lived in several places over the years, and our moves took us places we had not even visited before. Some said it was a leap of faith. Faith, yes; leap, no. We said as long as we are together, it doesn't matter where we live. It is fun to experience and explore different climates and surroundings. Very early in our relationship, we decided life together would never be dull. We knew it would not always be fun because life happens, but it has never been dull! We always look for the unique and venture beyond in order to experience life in the fullest. We never want to waste a minute of it, and we have never taken life, or each other, for granted. The experiences we have had throughout our life, make us who we are today.

Our life together has always been focused around airplanes. Aviation always has been, and always will be, a major part of our life. Sanford knew when he was quite young, he wanted to be a pilot. Then, two weeks after graduating high school, in the early 1970's, training began, and he became addicted to flying. He was exploring his aviation passion, and totally dedicated all his time and energy and money learning to fly.

Airplanes have opened up the world to us. We have seen and visited so many places that we would never have known about. The best part of all, we have gotten to meet, and become friends with, so many wonderful people. It's not the places you go, it's the people you meet.

Throughout our journeys, our Guardian Angels have always been there. Sometimes we did not realize it in the moment, sometimes we did. Faith is a wonderful thing, and we know someday all will be explained to us.

We dedicate this book to all our Guardian Angels.

Chapter 1

SUPER BREEZY – TIMES TWO

The Super Breezy. This is the one that started it all. Sanford had some ferry jobs here and there over the years, but this one put him on record as having the skill and experience and passion and will power to deliver. And deliver he did. Not only was this an airplane, it was extremely unique and not one that everyone could fly. The name 'Breezy' is an understatement for the description of this airplane.

We had just built our dream house in 2008, a hangar home in an airpark, and we were enjoying 'living with our airplane'. In early 2011, Sanford retired from his day job after over 24 years with the company. It was a fast paced, high stress job and retirement was exactly what he needed. At least, for three weeks, that is. Sanford found himself sitting in a chair in the front lawn, a .22 rifle in his lap, shooting mice and voles that were ruining his brand new, perfectly manicured lawn. Idle retirement was not in his wheelhouse.

Visits to the main airport were frequent for Sanford while I was still working full time. That's when the discussion came up about a brand-new airplane that needed to be delivered to Wisconsin. Sanford knew the builder, right there in Yakima, and offered to deliver the airplane. The builder, who has flown this type of airplane across the western region, said no, you don't want to do that, because cross-country flying on a Breezy is difficult, at best. Sanford insisted he did want to deliver the airplane, and explained to the builder that on day two or day three he would be wishing he had taken him up on the offer. The phone rang the next morning. "Sanford, the airplane will be ready to go this weekend. Come down tomorrow morning, and I will check you out in the airplane." Reality just arrived. Here we go.

The builder is a local friend and an expert in one-off and home-built, unique aircraft. While the airplane is considered experimental, it is a fully-performing, flying airplane. It was fitted with Super Cub wings and an IO-360 Lycoming 190 hp engine. It sported 31-inch bush tires, painted yellow, and finished with shiny diamond-patterned aluminum plating. The owners, father and son, had purchased a beautiful wooden, four-bladed pusher propeller twenty years before. They displayed the propeller on the wall in their home with the dream of someday putting it on a Breezy powerful enough to turn it. This meant the larger engine was needed, and the entire aircraft would need to be built bigger and stronger than the original design. Thus, the name 'Super' Breezy.

Their dream was going to become a reality. The Super Cub wings were shipped to Yakima along with the tail components. The specialized, custom engine rotated opposite of normal engines because it was a pusher instead of a tractor (puller). This made the torque factor on the propeller (called P-factor) the same as a normal aircraft. Their cherished propeller and engine, which was custom built by the father and son, were also sent to Yakima. Assembly had begun.

Months went by and the day finally arrived. All the pieces were assembled and it began to look like a flying machine from the early days of aviation. All the pilots in the area knew about the airplane, and it soon became widely known throughout the aviation community.

Sanford arrived the next morning to get checked out in the Super Breezy by the builder, and a small crowd has assembled to witness the first flight. The builder took her on the maiden voyage for a quick flight around the airport, even while the paint was still wet. While we all watched, Sanford could see the builder on the airplane waving his arms immediately after takeoff. We were listening on the radio to the conversation between the airport control tower and the pilot, and the pilot was not responding back to the tower. The control tower continued to give instructions to land, which the pilot followed, and he brought the airplane in for a beautiful landing. As the pilot, our friend and builder, arrived back, he was no longer wearing his flight headset, which is why he was not responding to the control tower. Sanford asked what happened, and the pilot said the headset kept coming off during flight, and he needed one hand to hang onto the headset while he flew the airplane with the other hand. You see, with the engine and propeller behind the pilot, any object that could get loose

would hit the propeller, doing tremendous damage. As a result, the pilot cannot carry anything that could come loose – a pen, an iPad or phone, not even a bottle of water. Nothing. All shirt and pant pockets had to be secured since there is no windshield or anything else in front of the pilot. Sanford even used safety wire on his pants legs so they would not ride up in the wind.

Our builder friend came up with a leather helmet, much like the pilots wore in the barnstormer days, although fitted for modern technology. It was built for an aviation headset so the pilot could have communication while in flight and could be securely fastened to his head. Sanford had installed his personal headset in the leather helmet and offered it to the builder to use. Sanford already had the dark brown bomber jacket, so all that was missing was a pair of goggles. Safety glasses would have to do.

Sanford is ready for the check ride. But things change. The builder had a student pilot show up, ready for his flight lesson. Knowing Sanford had the skill and experience, he told Sanford he was on his own, saying he didn't need a check out. Baptism by fire! Without missing a beat, Sanford pre-flighted the airplane, and logged into his memory where all the flight controls and switches were. Once in the pilot seat, the controls are not in view, so he had to memorize where each switch and control was so that he could reach them instinctively and without delay.

Here is Sanford's first-hand account of his first flight on the Super Breezy:

"With only one seatbelt holding me on (not in) and no shoulder harness, the buckle had just one click to it, so I had to be extremely careful to not accidentally release it. The next thing was to start the engine. All the controls were mounted under my seat, so I could not see any of the starting switches. I primed the engine and adjusted the mixture control and turned the key. The large engine behind me came to life. I had a small cluster of instruments on a console in front of me so I could monitor the engine's vital pressures and temperatures. Everything looks good for departure!

"As I keyed up the microphone to call for taxi instructions, I realized my mouth was as dry as a cotton ball, and I could not speak. I looked down and my knees were shaking violently. I hoped the crowd of on-lookers could not see them, and thought what have I gotten myself into now? I am scared to death of heights. But sitting inside a normal aircraft, I have no fear of heights.

"This was completely different. I had to get control of my fears and concentrate on the task before me. I swallowed hard and keyed up the microphone again, and made my request to the control tower. I was instructed to taxi to Runway 2-2. I changed to the tower frequency and let them know I was ready for takeoff. They immediately granted me clearance, which was a good thing so I didn't have a chance to change my mind. For the last time before takeoff, I turned my head and looked at the wing and tail controls to make sure they were in the proper position for takeoff. Then without moving the controls I put in full throttle and started picking up speed down the runway, steering with my feet.

"Suddenly I started to climb, but only about a foot. I realized I was sitting on top of the front tire and the main wheels were still on the runway. Then in another couple of hundred feet down the runway, the most amazing feeling I have ever experienced happened. The aircraft did not seem to climb, the earth just slipped away beneath me. The plan was to make a left circle around the airport and come in and land again. The control tower granted my request, and I was cleared to land. I began a very shallow, left bank to line up with the runway. Not being able to see the rest of the aircraft because it was all behind me, I had absolutely no way of knowing how much of a bank I was in. I could not look down below the horizon for fear of my acrophobia setting in. I started the turn to the left and estimated about a ten-degree bank.

"Things were working fine until I turned my head, and out of my peripheral vision, I could see the left-wing tip was in about a 45-degree bank. Not the mild ten-degree bank I was hoping for. I lifted the wing and made my turn as gentle as possible, all without looking below the horizon. I finally lined up with the runway, and I slowly reduced power. Without any instruments to tell me if I was climbing or descending, losing or gaining airspeed, I had to re-teach myself how to fly this airplane. If I felt more wind in my face, I  was descending and gaining airspeed. If I felt less wind, I had the stick pulled back too far, was climbing and starting to slow down, which would put me in a stall very soon. The challenge was to maintain the same amount of wind in my face and use the throttle to regulate my climb or descend rate. Here again, I had no feeling of descending. The runway just started to get closer and closer underneath me. Add a little power, take a little power out, add again…touchdown! Now let's do that two more times. The second and third flights had perfect landings, probably because I was zeroed in like a laser and would not let my fears creep in to my head.

"Once safely on the ground and back to parking, I pulled the mixture control to shut the engine down. The mechanic came over to me and asked me how it flew, and we discussed what adjustments needed to be done with the airplane. Without looking up, I heard someone from the crowd say, "Wow, those high-time pilots can fly anything." I never looked to see who said it for fear they could see the terror in my face. Show no fear!

"Many more testing flights followed. On one particular flight, I flew through a small rain shower that felt like a thousand needles hitting my face. I decided a face mask needed to be standard equipment on this aircraft."

I'm particularly fond of the face mask he is wearing – it has a skull on it! Long story, but we bought it the day before he left. Sanford needed something to cover his face from airborne items, such as bugs, sun, wind, and rain drops. It was a last-minute purchase at the local motorcycle shop, just before his initial departure, and it was the only one on the shelf. We had to have it, and we kept it, just in case…

Sanford's account of the cross-country trip:

"It was five of the most exciting and memorable days up to that point in my life for sure, flying over the mountains and the Midwest of the United States. To smell the pine trees and the many other smells that only a bird can experience. To fly over the top of a mountain covered with snow, only to surprise, and be surprised by, an elk sleeping in the sun. I never once thought of sophisticated electronic systems. This was a pure flying machine. I even got an opportunity to fly wing tip to wing tip with a red tail hawk, twice! It was truly a trip of a lifetime."

Then it happened again in the fall of 2016.

After this Super Breezy lived a very happy life in New York for five years, it was put up for sale and sold to a gentleman in Oregon. Sanford was contacted, by both the buyer and the seller, and asked to deliver it across the United States from the East Coast to the West Coast, a true transcontinental flight in this no-cockpit airplane. Sanford said this trip took eight wonderful days and recalls that he met some of the nicest people along the way he will never forget. He never understood why, but they all said he was crazy, for some reason.

Here is an account I wrote during Sanford's transcontinental trip:

Day One:

Sanford is off! He will once again be flying the Super Breezy, but this time he will bring it from KPEO Penn Yan, New York, to KHIO Hillsboro, Oregon to her new home! We are expecting a seven-or-eight-day trip with good weather.

Day Two:

Good morning! Sanford is delayed in New York due to weather and small mechanical issues. He is hoping to get a few more hours down the road yet today, but not sure about the weather, winds, and completing the repairs. He is at a very nice airport in the city of Olean, surrounded with great people loaning him tools and a courtesy car, which was an old police cruiser, to get to and from town. Things are good!

Days Three and Four:

After a couple of long days and cold temperatures at altitude, Sanford made it to Rapid City, South Dakota. Sanford has experienced significant temperature swings, so dressing for the occasion has been a challenge. He says the airplane has a great heater in it, but it is only ground-adjustable. He has to land the airplane and put on more clothes! His stop overnight yesterday was in Albert Lea, Minnesota – which is his hometown and where he learned to fly. In fact, the manager at the airport in Albert Lea notified the media of Sanford's arrival on the Super Breezy. As a result, one of the local television stations came out and did a story on his transcontinental flight.

Days Five and Six:

Sanford has made progress most of the way through Montana and will spend tonight in Missoula. He is hoping to make it to Yakima tomorrow. Sanford has been following Interstate 90 due to the rugged terrain as well as lower elevation through the mountain passes. Sanford really does not like to fly this close to major highways. He said it is really difficult to watch all the cars and trucks going faster than he is!

Things are going well, and the airplane is running great. Temperatures at altitude are cold, as well as the mornings, so he has been delayed the last two days, waiting for it to warm up. We are expecting near 90° in Yakima tomorrow, so hoping he enjoys some warmer temperatures as he crosses the mountains and heads this way. Then if all goes well one more day to KHIO Hillsboro, Oregon, to the Super Breezy's new home!

Sanford's account on Day Seven:

"It looks like everyone who bet against me may have to pay up. I think I'm going to make it. I am now at home with one more leg to go in a day or two once it quits raining in Portland, Oregon. What a trip – I am truly blessed to have met such fine people in my life.

"I am back in Yakima where it all started. My life has been a trip since I first saw this aircraft. I have, in the past, closed my eyes and wondered what lies between here and there. At a slow mile a minute, and a low altitude, stopping often, and adding a bit of adrenaline — now I know!

"I have seen New York maple trees that make my pancakes taste sweet and delicious. Grazed the south side of Lake Erie. Saw the industrial cities of Fort Wayne, Indiana and Chicago. Flown over Iowa corn fields and bean fields. Over the top of Blue Earth, Minnesota, where the Jolly Green Giant grows my green beans. Had the fun of putting the run on those rascally coyotes. Watched as the antelope raced across the prairies. To increase the power and climb over a mountain peak just to discover a herd of elk sunning themselves away from everyone but me. Watch a moose that was enjoying his swamp-grass dinner.

"If I climbed too high, I could see too far ahead which made it seem like I was not making any progress. What I could see on the horizon was more than an hour away and felt like I would never get there. If I flew low, it gave me a ground rush – the feeling I was moving much faster. However, if I flew near the freeway, it was a psychological thing when I saw cars and semi-trucks passing me. The speed limit on the freeway across Montana is 80 mph. The reason I know this is because I could read the speed limit signs!

"I turned and started cutting across the plains, and I happened upon a wagon trail that the settlers must have traveled when they came west. Straight as an arrow for miles and miles. The road had been cut in through the small hills and creeks, clearly showing the way west. As I flew along the trail at an altitude of ten feet or so, I imagined what it must have been like for them to drive the wagons or walk or ride horses. If they got sick or hurt, it must have been awful to ride in a wagon with no suspension to ease the rough trail. I could now appreciate how fast 70 miles an hour was, plus riding on a cushion of air. Thinking of all the people that made this journey years ago, I never again thought of myself flying slow, because it sure beats riding a horse!

"As I entered the Rocky Mountains, I needed to climb to a higher altitude for safe passage. At that altitude, the temperature was 44° and I could see it snowing on top of the mountain. I was struggling to stay warm, so I pulled my heavy leather coat down to help keep my back warm. In doing so, I accidentally snagged the seatbelt buckle and released the seatbelt. With a belt dangling in the wind on each side of me, I had to make a decision. Do I let go of the controls and grab the seatbelts? Or do I just hang on for dear life and hope a gust of wind doesn't buck me out of the chair? Decisions, decisions, decisions!

"Now racing the sun, exhausted and cold, I increased the throttle and told myself: I must go faster, I must go faster! I was headed to my final destination for the day at an airport with a control tower. When I was only seven miles away from the airport, I realized at my last stop I attached my leather helmet strap over the top of my microphone on my headset. Not good! I removed my glove from one hand and tried to pull the microphone out from underneath the strap. Then to my horror, I pulled off the foam muff covering the microphone, which eliminates wind noise. Without it, the control tower could not understand me. With it pinched tightly in my fingers, I thought now what am I going to do with it in this 70 mph wind? I carefully opened up my jacket and placed the foam muff up in my right arm pit and zipped my coat shut.

So here I am, no gloves on, no way to call the control tower, what am I going to do? Only one thing I could think of. I looked down and found a gravel road, landed, got my stuff together, took off again, and within one minute I keyed up the microphone to say: "November Seven Zero Zero Papa Yankee, seven miles to the east landing with the numbers." Problem solved.

"Another thing that I did not realize was how many friends I have all across this country, because everyone was waving at me as I passed overhead. But the best thing I've seen on my whole trip was the smile on my wife's face when I arrived home!"

After a couple of days in Yakima waiting for weather and getting some much-needed sleep and TLC, Sanford invited me to ride along on his final day to deliver the Super Breezy to Hillsboro. I jumped at the chance! Even though it was less than a four-hour drive from our house, it took most of the day to fly her to her new home. After leaving our home in Yakima, we flew southwest toward the Washington / Oregon border along the Columbia River.

Flying along the river, we could see a wall of rain ahead of us where the river narrowed near Hood River, Oregon. We stopped for fuel and to assess the weather, because the Super Breezy is not made to fly in rain… and neither are we! Sanford decided to continue west and fly toward the rain to see if there was a break that we could sneak through. Sure enough, a bright spot, along with good timing, and we were through. We did get a bit of rain – wait, let me correct that. Sanford got some rain in his face, but I ducked behind him and stayed completely dry! There are advantages to being the passenger.

Sunshine and good weather were ahead of us for the remainder of the trip. Sanford safely and successfully delivered the Super Breezy again. And I got to experience the exciting hand-off of a treasured airplane to its new owner. Just for the record, I'm hooked on flying on (not in) this airplane!

Soon after Sanford arrived home, he wrote this heart-warming letter to a community he encountered on his way west with the Super Breezy. It was such a memorable and welcoming community, and Sanford has many fond memories of his short stay there. His letter was published in their local newspaper a few days later.

Honorable William J. Aiello
Mayor, City of Olean

Dear Mayor Aiello,

I would like to thank you and the people of Olean, particularly the nice people I met at your beautiful airport.

I am a ferry pilot and I deliver airplanes across North America. A recent delivery took me on a transcontinental journey across the United States on a no-cockpit airplane called a Super Breezy. Seated on a chair with only one seat belt and no windshield and totally exposed to the wind and weather, I had an unlimited view in all directions. Flying over the beautiful rolling hills of New York, admiring the maple trees and the beautiful landscape, I was drawn to one of the nicest looking airports I had ever seen in my life. It was quite obvious that the people managing the airport took great pride in taking care of it. For this reason alone, I had to land and meet these people.

After inspecting the aircraft before departure, I determined I had some small maintenance issues that I needed to tend to before I continued on my trip to the West Coast. While working on the aircraft, inside the hangar with rain and drizzle just over the hills outside, someone said to me, you're not having a good day are you? I responded to the gentleman, I am inside and dry. Everyone at this airport is so kind and helpful, they have loaned me tools and supplies I need. I have a cup of coffee in my hand, a courtesy car to drive to town, reservations at a very nice hotel tonight with a great restaurant right next to it. I told him, allow me to introduce myself. You are looking at the luckiest person you have ever met in your life. I have been flying airplanes for 43 years now. Trust me when I say one of the worst things is to be far, far away from home and all alone with an aircraft needing repairs. I could not ask for more hospitality and help from the nicest people I have met here. I was also lucky enough to be here for your wonderful flight breakfast before I continued west.

I have shared my experience with several pilots and encouraged them to come and visit your beautiful airport and town. Please know and understand how important your airport is to your community. I am looking forward to returning and reuniting with my friends from Olean.

Thank you,
Sanford Reim

Chapter 2

THE INTRODUCTION

I was living in Des Moines, Iowa, paying attention to living, working, and figuring out where and how to move to a new location and make a fresh start. I was born and raised there, and realized one day this was not the way I wanted to live. I was working Monday through Friday at a local television station in the commercial sales department. We were in the downtown area which had many drawbacks, but I loved my job. I just wasn't getting ahead and making the changes and improvements like I had dreamed. So, I got a second job in the evenings and weekends, and then a third during my lunch hours during the week. I was determined to get ahead and make some major changes and turned my focus entirely on working and saving money.

On a free afternoon I was visiting with my neighbors just a couple doors down in the mobile home park where I was living. I owned my trailer, and I felt good about that. But it was still a mobile home park that required paying lot rent and living under the owners' rules and regulations. It kept the neighborhood clean and with mostly good people, so that was good, but it still had restrictions that I wanted to be free of.

Back to talking with my neighbors. Wonderful people, a few years older than me, doing the same, working hard trying to get ahead. In talking with them about work, my neighbor came up with an idea. He wanted to introduce me to a new guy at work that was also single and fairly new to the area. He had moved down from Minnesota for a better job and was doing the same as me, working as much as possible to get ahead and make some changes.

My neighbor was working hard at a second job too – to set us up on a blind date. I was busy and tired of the dating scene, and was hesitant. But the more my neighbor talked about his friend at work, the more interested I became. After all, he drove a Jeep, was a pilot, and owned his own airplane.

One Sunday afternoon my neighbor invited his friend over for dinner. He told me about it the day before, and said to watch for a silver Jeep parked at his house. I was a little excited about meeting someone totally new and not from the area. So not knowing exactly what time to be available, I decided it was a good time to get some exercise and go for a ride on my bicycle around the neighborhood. Several laps later (I got a lot of exercise that afternoon), there was the Jeep! I slowed down and passed by to take a look at the driver. That turned out to not be so easy, because he was sitting crossways in the front seats, sound asleep! My neighbor was not home yet, and his friend arrived early, so time to take a nap. Later I found out the crazy hours and long days these guys worked and now understood grabbing a little shuteye whenever you can was a bonus.

Later in the day, as I kept a watchful eye on my neighbor's house, they were outside enjoying the nice weather. Another ride on my bicycle was in order. Taking the long way around I came across the guys walking and stopped for an introduction. I nearly fell over. Those piercing blue eyes and that Minnesota twang. I knew then and there I had to get to know more about this handsome guy named Sanford!

Over the next few weeks we talked on the phone when our schedules allowed. Sanford was out of town a lot with an erratic schedule, so planning a day and time when he was in town was tough. And when he was in town, it was time to catch up on family, mail, paying bills, shopping, etc. But we were able to catch a movie together one Sunday afternoon. It was a matinee so tickets were cheap, $.99 in fact, and the movie was Chariots of Fire. It was supposed to be an Academy Award winning movie, but oddly I don't remember much of it.

After the movie we decided to get a pizza and coffee and have a chance to talk. One of the bonuses of working at the television station is the advertisers sometimes traded their product for commercial time. In this case, Pizza Hut traded $10 coupons, which were often shared with employees. So off to Pizza Hut for a wonderful evening and good pizza. It turns out the pizza was $10 and included the coffee, so the bill was about $.32 plus tip. One could say I was a cheap date.

After this date I realized for sure that Sanford was 'the one' and that love at first sight really happens. I had just needed a little more confirmation since I was trying to be cautious. But it was overwhelming, and I was head over heels for this guy.

A few weeks later Sanford invited me to his company Christmas party, which I gladly accepted. It was at a hotel banquet room with about 30 to 40 people attending. A wonderful evening of friends and food and Christmas spirit was ending too soon. Once the dinner was over, several of the group decided to head to the country-western bar for some music and dancing. Sanford asked me if I wanted to go to the bar, too. My mind was racing on what to say, because I really wanted to spend some time alone with him since we saw each other so infrequently. My response was: "Honestly?" And he said: "Yes, always." I told him I wanted to spend more time with just him, and he asked what I wanted to do. I said: "Take me flying." He immediately responded: "Let's go!"

It was a Saturday night, mid-December, with snow on the ground, and a cold but clear night. I had not flown in a small airplane before, so it was an entirely new experience. We drove to the airport, both of us excited about going flying. It was, and still is, Sanford's passion to fly. And I wanted to see him in his true element. Shortly after midnight, the engine was running and we were taxiing onto the runway. The stars were out and I was in an adventure beyond my wildest dreams.

After takeoff, Sanford called the airport tower and asked for clearance to fly into their airspace. They put us 5,000 feet and gave permission to fly a ten-mile square pattern around the city. The city lights were amazing, and the Christmas lights were magnificent! Not only did we go flying, we also saw something that could only be experienced in an airplane. I began to understand his passion.

Two hours later we landed at the main airport to take a break and refuel the airplane. The night worker at the service center was thrilled to have company and something to do. We had a cup of coffee and got a tour of one of the hangars with million-dollar private jets. It was a whole new world that I got to see that night, both on land and in the air.

We flew back to the airport where he kept his airplane and tucked it away. It was getting close to breakfast time and we realized we had been together all night, talking and sharing our dreams and priorities. They were the same. We decided life was not going to be dull together.

And the rest is history, as they say. That was over 37 years ago, and we just celebrated our 34th wedding anniversary. Our life together has never been dull, either! Life sometimes happens, and you deal with that. But the world of aviation has opened up so many opportunities for us. I admire Sanford for his hard work of getting and keeping his pilot's license, getting more and better license ratings, and always improving his skills. Plus owning an airplane is an important responsibility. Maintenance has to be over the top. No cheap fixes or saying I'll get to it next week. The reward is tremendous and we are both passionate about our airplanes. They have carried us near and far and always brought us home safely.

We truly have been blessed!

Chapter 3

Bush-Wacking

Not sure if you have ever heard this term. It might be a Midwest thing. When we were teenagers, we were always looking for some fun on a warm summer Saturday night. If we didn't have a date, we figured we should mess with somebody that did. Bush-wacking was the thing. Basically, the fun was to sneak up on a couple in a parked car, after dark, usually in a park or a back road, then turn on the headlights, honk the horn, and drive off hooting and hollering and laughing. Amazing how much fun we used to be able to have late at night, and didn't have to be scared about being out after dark.

Sanford and I were still dating, and I loved to fly with him. We were both living in Iowa at the time, and summers were nice there with beautiful evenings just around sunset. We had gone on a day trip in the Cessna 150 that he owned at the time, a two-seater, and enjoyed a late breakfast in one of the several Amana Colonies in Central Iowa. They were famous for their restaurants that served home-style meals that included their home-grown meats and vegetables. One of the main

Colonies had a beautiful grass airstrip about two blocks away from the main street, so it was an easy walk and fun to spend the day shopping and visiting their factories.

Furniture was hand made at the Amana Colonies. It was some of the most beautiful furniture we have ever seen and made with heirloom quality. Part of the furniture factory was a cuckoo clock factory and showroom that had the most intricate and decorative clocks. I loved to walk through there and see all the different styles and different characters they had in the clocks that came out to cuckoo. They also had a woolen mill and retail store that offered beautiful locally-made clothes and sweaters of quality that would nearly last forever.

After spending most of the day there, we walked back to the airplane to head home. The airport where Sanford kept the airplane was about an hour flight, and it was situated between two corn fields just off a highway outside of Des Moines. Our route to fly to and from the Amana Colonies was pretty much parallel to Interstate 80, running east and west through Iowa.

We were about half way home, flying a couple thousand feet in the air, right at sunset. It was a beautiful evening, and we were enjoying the smooth flight. That's when I spotted them. I noticed a car, with the headlights on, driving down a gravel road toward the freeway. But the road was a dead end with only corn fields on either side. It was one of many roads that were cut off when the freeway was built years ago, and it seemed odd that a car would be driving there with nowhere to go.

They slowed down, and then stopped. Then the car backed about 30 feet off the road onto a field entrance, stopped, and shut off the headlights. Although Sanford and I had not yet talked much about either of our teenage days, I looked at him, pointed at the car, and said: "Bushwacking?" He instantly grinned and said: "Hang on."

Sanford pulled the power back in the airplane so we could quietly descend. He made a big circle over the field, keeping an eye on the car which had not moved. We were just about down to a low enough altitude over the corn field as Sanford lined up behind the car. Still flying at reduced power, we were nearly quiet as a mouse. At one point we could see through the back window out the windshield, since the field was lower than the road. It appeared the car was empty since we could not see anyone sitting up.

As we came up on the car, slightly off to the side and above, Sanford brought in full power. We went from stealth to roaring just as we flew past the car. Sanford left full power in as we flew across the road and over the next corn field. We turned and climbed to a higher altitude so we could see if they were still in the car. As we watched, the doors never opened. But the headlights came on, and the car pulled out of the field back on to the gravel road, spinning tires and making so much dust we could no longer see the car.

We watched that cloud of dust for a long way wondering if they would ever figure out who just bush-wacked them!

Chapter 4

First Fly-In Fishing Trip

Sanford and I had been married less than a year when he took a job transfer and we moved from Des Moines, Iowa, to Northern Minnesota. Sanford started his new position in International Falls the first of November that year, and I moved up there about four weeks later on Thanksgiving weekend. While Sanford was there, he found us a place to rent until we could buy a house.

A couple months earlier, while we were still living in Des Moines, I will always remember the moment Sanford called me at work and asked me: "How much do you like your job?" It was a Friday afternoon and Sanford had been watching the job postings at his work for an opening in Minnesota, his home state. We had decided that we wanted to move out of Iowa at the earliest opportunity, and when Sanford asked me where I wanted to move to in Minnesota, I said anywhere north of Minneapolis. We had taken a short vacation over Memorial Day weekend a couple years before, which was my first fly-in fishing trip.

Sanford was born and raised in Albert Lea, Minnesota, where his folks still lived at the time. He had an aunt and uncle living up north in Bemidji, and his folks had gone up to see them for a few days. They drove their pickup and pulled the boat so they could fish on Upper Red Lake, where there was supposed to be great walleye fishing. I had heard so much about it, and I had never been fishing for walleye. And I do love to fish. We decided to fly his Cessna 150 up to Bemidji rather than drive. We loaded the airplane with a couple suitcases and his tackle box, which had the airplane packed to the ceiling. It was just a two-seater and a small luggage area, so it didn't take much to fill it.

We left after work one evening and made the flight to Southern Minnesota the first night. We planned to stay at his folks' house overnight, and make the rest of the trip early the next morning. We landed late in the evening at the Albert Lea airport, and caught a ride to the house from one of the airport mechanics. Sanford called his sister, who lived a few miles down the road, and asked her to pick us up at the house at 6:00 am and give us a ride to the airport the next morning. We were ready to call it a night, and Sanford set the alarm on his digital watch (which was new technology at the time) for 5:00 am so we could be up and ready to go when she got there.

Sanford and I had only been together a little more than a year, and I had not yet met his family, including his sister. I was looking forward to meeting her and would soon be meeting his folks and aunt and uncle in Bemidji. But I have to admit, I was more excited about flying and fishing.

Next thing I know, the back door flies open, the lights come on, and Sanford's sister is standing in the doorway with a great big grin on her face. We missed the alarm and overslept, and his sister was gleefully pleased at waking us up. No time like the present to do introductions, so as Sanford was getting up and heading to the shower, he did the honors. I was mortified! There I was, squinting and rubbing my eyes, and meeting my soon-to-be sister-in-law. All I could do was say hi and pull the covers over my head.

We had a beautiful flight the rest of the way to Bemidji. The landscape north of Minneapolis changes from heavily-populated areas, becoming more rural and covered with trees and lakes. The pine trees are a gorgeous dark green and mixed with several varieties of hardwood trees. The lakes were clean with clear blue water, and the further north we flew, the prettier it became.

Since this was before cell phones, Sanford used a unique way to let his folks know we were about to land and we needed a ride. He would fly over the house a time or two until they came outside. Once they were standing in the yard, he would make one more pass, pull the power back on the engine, open the window and shout: "Come pick us up at the airport." A few minutes later, we were on the ground. I remember my first few steps out of the airplane on the tarmac at the Bemidji airport. It was a sunny, nice day with a slight breeze. The air was amazing. It was fresh and clean and I could smell the pine trees. There were lakes everywhere. I fell in love with Northern Minnesota right then and there.

We unloaded the airplane and everyone arrived to pick us up. Introductions were done, a little more formal than with his sister, and we were on the way to his aunt and uncle's house.

We borrowed the folks' pickup and boat and fishing poles and planned to spend the weekend at Upper Red Lake. We also needed to borrow cooking and camping equipment, and his aunt fixed us up with all we needed. We were under strict orders, though, to be sure and bring back the cast iron frying pan she loaned us. She received it as a wedding gift nearly fifty years before, and it was her favorite frying pan. We were honored.

This was all new to me. Taking a trip in the airplane, camping and fishing on a huge lake, and a whole new kind of fishing. We drove to a place called Waskish, which was the public access to Upper Red Lake. The campground was nice and we parked right alongside the river that fed into the lake. The fish cleaning house was at one end of the campground, and the biffies were at the other end. We unloaded the boat and Sanford drove it around and tied it to shore, just behind where we were camped. His dad's pickup had a canopy on the back and he had built a full-size shelf inside. The top was for sleeping and under was storage for the camping gear. The tailgate was the table and prep site, and we found a couple of tree stumps to use for seats around the fire. We were all set and headed out for some fishing.

I love the outdoors and thought I was ready to go. It was Memorial Day weekend, which I was used to being the start of summer. I packed light, especially since we traveled in the airplane. I had a t-shirt, long-sleeve shirt, sweater, and jacket in case it rained. I was all set.

Then Minnesota taught me a lesson. It was windy and rainy and cold. I wore all my clothes, all the time, the whole weekend. Out in the boat, the lake was rough in my opinion, but Sanford called it the perfect walleye chop. He would motor past the point where he wanted to fish, line us up with the wind, and shut the engine off. We would drift back and bounce the fishing lures along the bottom since that's where the walleyes were. I grew up on bobber fishing, so this was a new technique for me. Every time I would bounce off a rock on the bottom, I thought I had a bite. After a few passes and no luck, Sanford gave me a few tips. I would let the sinker hit the bottom again but not pull it up each time, thinking it would bounce along the bottom. Wrong. Now I was getting snagged nearly every pass and lost the tackle a couple of times, too.

This really hurt my pride. I thought I was a pretty good fisherman for a girl since I had always fished growing up. After a few passes over his favorite fishing hole, Sanford had already bagged five or six nice fish, and I was still trying not to get snagged. On top of losing my tackle and being out-fished, I kept losing my minnow. I was having trouble getting the minnow on the hook properly so it would not get knocked off on the rocks. You see, I was working in downtown offices and had spare time in the evenings, not doing much manual labor, and I found I could grow and polish very nice, very long, fingernails. I quickly realized long fingernails and baiting fish hooks just did not work. Something had to change. A couple minutes later and a pair of fingernail clippers, problem solved. It was the very next pass over the fishing hole when I caught my first walleye!

Later that evening, after a wonderful supper of fresh fish, fried potatoes, and baked beans (better known in Minnesota as shore lunch), we took a walk around the campground with a cup of coffee to enjoy the clear night skies. Since I grew up in the city, I had never seen such a night sky with no light pollution to dim it out. In total wonder and amazement, I quickly found the big dipper, then the little dipper. I found the three stars on Orion's Belt, although I couldn't remember how to make out the rest of the constellation. Then I noticed something strange. There was a band of some kind of white-wash going across the sky. I asked Sanford if he knew what that was. He looked at me, kind of strange, and told me what it was. I didn't believe him and thought he was pranking me, and told him that was just a fairy tale. Sanford swore it was the truth, and it was.

Here I am, with the love of my life, approaching 30 years old, gazing at the most amazing sky I had ever seen, and I just discovered the Milky Way. Wow!

Chapter 5

FINDING THE FLOATS

While living in Iowa, Sanford decided to sell his Cessna 150 that I referred to as a cream puff. It was well maintained, had great paint and interior, and we trusted it totally. But we wanted to do more with our flying, and we needed more room and more power. The airplane sold right away, so now the hunt was on for a new airplane.

It is very common for people to purchase an airplane that is not located close by. That is the reason Sanford stays busy delivering airplanes. Most are newly purchased and the owner needs to retrieve it. Sometimes the owners are not familiar with the airplane and ask Sanford to deliver it so they can take lessons from a local instructor. Some owners are not familiar with the seasonal weather and mountainous terrain, and need a skilled and experienced pilot to make the journey. No matter the reasons, Sanford has had countless cross-country flights moving airplanes to their new homes.

We owned a hangar at a small grass airport about 20 miles south of Des Moines. We were in a building that had four separate hangars, and ours had a dirt floor with no door. It faced south, so it got good sun and warmth in the winter and suited our needs, providing shelter from the elements. It was now empty and needed a new tenant. Sanford had set his sights on a specific airplane – a Cessna 170. As luck would have it, he found it, right at the same airport! Sanford contacted the owner, made the deal, and we literally rolled it across the grass runway and into our hangar! We still own the airplane and fly it every chance we get.

After moving to Northern Minnesota, we fitted our Cessna 170 with floats so we could truly enjoy the Land of 10,000 Lakes. When we bought the airplane, Sanford had the goal of making it a floatplane, but it had never been fitted with floats before. When it was built in 1952, a factory float kit was installed, which was very unique and rare. It included reinforcements where the float struts fitted into the fuselage, lifting rings on the top of the fuselage to raise the airplane on a hoist, and anti-corrosion undercoating throughout the wings and tail section of the airplane. We had a lot of work to do in the meantime, and we set a long-term goal of about ten years.

Several items had to be addressed before we would be able to enjoy float flying at its finest. We needed a bigger and more powerful engine. To find one was one thing, but to find a mechanic skilled enough to make the changes and modifications was another. Then there was the paperwork needed to make it legal for both the FAA and the insurance company. That's when Christmas came right at Christmas! Early in Sanford's flying career, he had just gotten his license and doing as much flying as he could, and he worked for an entrepreneur that had several businesses going at once. Sanford drove gravel truck some days, he helped work on airplanes some days, and other days he helped retrieve airplanes that his boss had just purchased to rebuild and resell. This is where Sanford gained his experience flying many different airplanes.

Now we are on our way to see Sanford's family and celebrate Christmas together. We stopped along the way to say hello to his old boss, who had also become a good friend. As chance would have it, his boss had another Cessna 170 like ours, a few years newer, with the larger and more powerful engine we needed. Sanford got the keys and we took it for a flight. A few minutes later, we made the deal to swap the engines on the airplanes, firewall forward, and had a very skilled airplane mechanic to do the job with every scrap of paperwork we needed to be legal.

Before installation of the floats, we needed to keep working on the rest of the things on our list. We needed to upgrade the radios and gauges in the airplane. Sanford also needed to get his float rating from a certified instructor. Luckily, there was one in a town about 80 miles away and had a floatplane available for instruction. Sanford took a few days off work and accomplished his rating. I will never forget when he returned home with that great big smile on his face!

Now we needed to find floats for our Cessna. There were only two that were approved and certified for our airplane, but Sanford felt one of the sizes was too small. We set our sights on the larger set called PK Floats. Hunting high and low on all the aviation sites to try and buy a used set of floats proved to be fruitless. After more than a year of searching, Sanford found contact information for the company that now owned the manufacturing rights to the PK Floats. After contacting them, we found out why we could not find a used set for our airplane. There had only been five sets ever built and fitted onto our model of Cessna, so they were most likely non-existent. Buying brand new floats was our only option.

The design on these floats started out in a very small town in Northern Minnesota called International Falls, where we lived at the time. A local resident designed, patented, and built floats for smaller airplanes, such as Aeronca Champs and Piper Cubs. His name was Peter Kelner, as in PK Floats. He had sold the patent to another company years before located in Sanford, Maine. A town called Sanford…ironic. Now out of business, the patent was acquired by a company in Albuquerque, New Mexico. We contracted with them to build a set of floats for us, and a road trip was in our near future. We had now gone full circle on PK Floats, bringing them back to their birthplace. And the other ironic thing, Peter Kelner's daughter lived right across the street from us. We were also lucky enough to bump into Peter Kelner one afternoon, while parking the Cessna at the dock of a local resort. He was thrilled to see the larger design of his floats that still carries his initials and emblem.

Now we are getting close to the floats being completed at the factory. We still had four major things to get done on the airplane before installation: Get our annual maintenance inspection done, have the airplane wings re-skinned (more on that in a moment), re-paint the airplane, and a road trip from Northern Minnesota to New Mexico.

A few months before, we suffered through an unbelievable summer thunderstorm that produced high winds and hail. The winds were clocked at 67 mph and hail stones 3-1/2 inches in diameter. To add insult to injury, the hail stones were jagged and irregular shaped, showing hundreds of tiny hail stones had fused and frozen together to create these destructive monstrosities. Not only did it do tremendous damage to ours and other airplanes, it also destroyed the roof on our house. We diverted our attention to working with the insurance companies to get things repaired as quickly as possible. Part of that was having the tops of the wings re-skinned to look brand new. And as long as we were repairing the wings, we decided to install a STOL kit – Short Take Off and Landing. The kit was designed to increase the wings' efficiency and provide resistance to stalls and spins. It would also help us to fly slower but still safely, allowing us to land on the water at a much slower speed. This helped us several times when we had no choice but to land on rough water.

The floats are complete and now it is time for the road trip. We borrowed a flat-bed trailer from a friend, which was actually a four-place snowmobile trailer. It worked perfect. But these floats were a big investment for us so I wanted insurance. I called our auto insurance, and they said no because they were not in an enclosed trailer. I called our airplane insurance, and they said no because they were unassembled and uninstalled. I called our homeowners insurance, and they just laughed. No way to get insurance for either damage or theft. The road trip turned into two full days' driving to Albuquerque, and 26 straight hours to drive back since we could not secure or protect the brand-new floats.

The employees at the factory were wonderful. They were highly skilled and took pride in their work. They wanted to make sure these floats made the journey safely and without a scratch. It didn't take long for them to come up with a plan to mount the floats on the trailer. They decided to turn them upside down and fashioned two long 2 x 4's by rounding the edges so that they would fit through the spreader bar fittings. Then they stacked and mounted three short pieces of 2 x 4's on each and secured the long boards to them. This design suspended the floats above the bed of the trailer. Then they fashioned toe-blocks to keep the floats from sliding sideways and secured them to the long boards. As I said before, it worked perfect. But we still needed to cover them to protect them from road debris. We brought along a large blue tarp that we draped over the floats, putting duct tape over the sharp corners so it would not tear in the wind. The tarp was about two feet too short, so we left the backs of the floats exposed at the very back of the trailer. There was little chance they would suffer any damage.

On the journey home, we encountered several vehicles that would start to pass us on the freeway, only to slow down and match our speed as they were alongside the trailer. Looking intently at the items under the blue tarp, we wondered what they must have concluded they were. In taking a second look, from their perspective, we decided they looked like a couple of homemade torpedoes! One of the vehicles that took a long, hard look on the freeway was a state trooper. Expecting that he might pull us over, even to just ask what the cargo was, he finally sped up and pulled away, never looking at us in the car as he went by.

Sanford always likes to sample the local cuisine at restaurants when he is traveling, and he asks what they recommend we try while we are visiting their city. When we traveled to the Pacific Northwest the first time, we sampled their famous Dungeness crab, served chilled with fresh garlic and butter. When we visited Florida, they recommended stone crab, which was out of this world. When we visited New Mexico, we found an authentic Mexican restaurant, and lucky for us it was during their Cinco de Mayo celebration. It was wonderful!

On our 26-hour marathon drive home with the floats, we drove through Denver, Colorado. At about 10:00 pm at night, we stopped in Denver for a late-night supper. Can you guess what Sanford had? A Denver omelette. As we were paying the bill, the cashier said to me: "Okay, we've all been guessing and can't figure out what you guys have on the trailer. What is it?" My initial response was we worked for the government and could not divulge that information. But, alas, I cannot keep a straight face. I fessed up and told her they were floats, or pontoons, for our airplane, laying upside down. I could hear: "Oh, wow, okay, never would have guessed" from about six people at the café counter along with the cashier, all at the same time.

Three months earlier, Sanford had made an appointment with our airplane mechanic to bring in our Cessna and install the new floats. It was scheduled on a Wednesday in May, and Sanford had told him we would be driving back from New Mexico with the floats on the trailer and expect us around noon. We decided to drop off the airplane on our way to Albuquerque, but we found out we could not land at his grass air strip. The ground was too wet and soft from the winter thaw. We had to land at the main airport, which was a few miles down the road. Our mechanic said no problem, that he could retrieve the airplane and transport it to his shop using his pickup. He would drop the tailgate and load the tail of the airplane onto the tailgate. He would then drive the roads from the main airport to his shop, and had help with him to make sure they would clear trees and branches and road signs. This was common practice for him, and he had worked with the city years before to lower the street signs and other obstructions just for this purpose.

On that Wednesday morning of our appointment to deliver the floats, we were just a few miles away from the mechanic's shop at about 10:30 am. We were going to make our appointment; in fact, we were going to be early. Just as we were making the final turn to arrive, we were stunned to see our airplane in the middle of the road! The mechanic thought there was no way we would be back by then, but felt he should go ahead and have the airplane on site, just in case. Timing is everything, and now it was time for a parade! We happily followed our airplane down the road while it was being towed backwards, looking at us!

A few days later our dream came true. We were ready for her maiden voyage on floats. It was a perfect day, and Sanford did a masterful job. We not only launched the airplane for the first time on floats, we launched a whole new part of our life in aviation. And it has been more fun than should be allowed! We achieved our ten-year goal of putting floats on the airplane, and accomplished it in just over eight years. As of this writing, we still proudly own this airplane and floats and snow skis, 34 years and counting!

Chapter 6

THANKS, BUT NO THANKS!

Years ago, Sanford got his first job as a ferry pilot in Northern Minnesota. It was a Cessna 206 floatplane on straight floats – no wheels underneath the floats so it could only land on water. It needed to be transported from Ontario, Canada, to the Minneapolis, Minnesota, area. We were living in International Falls at the time, and winter was fast approaching. Once winter weather sets in, we're in it for the next several months. Time was of the essence.

The owner found a Canadian bush pilot to pick up and deliver the airplane from the Ontario area to the Minnesota border. That's all the further the pilot would take it since he was not familiar flying in the States, let alone in controlled airports and the airspace around them. He parked it on the Minnesota shoreline of Rainy Lake at a pilot friend's house in our hometown, and the owner needed an experienced pilot with the proper license ratings, float time experience, bush flying experience, and the technical knowledge and experience to fly into airport-controlled zones. That was Sanford.

We drove out to the airplane to give it a check out and pre-flight inspection. Sanford wanted to fly it locally just to make sure all was good for the remaining flight to Minneapolis. It was a beautiful evening and the lake waters were calm and flat. We both hopped in and took her for a spin. What a great flying airplane. Sanford is all set to leave Saturday to deliver the airplane.

The next evening Sanford called our local pilot friend where the Cessna was parked on the lake to let him know he was planning an early morning departure on Saturday. After talking with him for a few minutes, our pilot friend told Sanford the Canadian pilot had some trouble fueling the airplane and that the pilot had also complained about how hard it was to get the Cessna to take off the water. This Cessna had four fuel tanks – two in each of the wings and all with separate fuel caps. The Canadian pilot could not get the fuel caps off the outboard secondary tanks, so he only filled the two inboard main tanks.

Since it had been a relatively short flight on the Canadian side, Sanford thought there should be enough remaining fuel to go the distance to Minneapolis, but he checked to make sure after having flown the airplane the evening before. Sanford also said he figured the Canadian pilot had not used wing flaps and good float flying technique for takeoff to help break the suction the floats create on water. Fuel and takeoff problems solved.

The floats can create a suction on the water as the airplane accelerates for takeoff. The faster you go, the more suction the floats can create, so you need something to break that suction. Sometimes a ripple on the surface of the water will do, and sometimes it takes a little more ingenuity and finesse and skill by the pilot. There is a technique that Sanford uses that takes advantage of the aerodynamics of the airplane and floats, and the force of the engine and propeller.

Back to Sanford's phone conversation. Our local pilot friend had come to his own conclusion that there must be some fuel in the two outboard tanks. And now that the two inboard tanks were full, it must have made the airplane too heavy and caused the difficulty of taking off the water. And since friends are here to help, and pilots always help other pilots, he and a buddy decided to siphon fuel out of the two inboard main tanks to help lighten the load. I distinctly remember hearing Sanford's side of the phone call at this point: "What!? What!? You did what!? You need to put that fuel back in the airplane! …What? You already dumped it into your own airplanes?" Sanford quickly finished the phone call, looked at me and said: "Let's go."

We jumped in our pickup, which had a fuel tank in the back that we used for our own floatplane, and headed to the lake. Sanford checked the fuel level in both the two outboard and two inboard wing tanks. The two outboard tanks were completely empty! And sure enough, with the reduced amount of fuel remaining in the two inboard main tanks, he calculated he would have been about 30 minutes short of his destination in Minneapolis when he ran out of fuel. We filled the tanks back up, Sanford recalculated the fuel again, and determined it was sufficient to make the trip. That was a close call. Pilots and friends are here to help. But this time, thanks, but no thanks!

Now it's Friday and the plan was to leave Saturday morning. Sanford had been watching the weather forecast all week and it was not looking good. Then Friday morning the prediction got worse with colder temperatures, low clouds, freezing rain, and snow starting early Saturday. That was a no-go. Sanford decided he needed to leave right away Friday afternoon if he was going to get this airplane to Minneapolis before winter set in, or the next chance would be next spring. Plus, the airplane could not be left in the lake all winter since the lake freezes over and the area gets a lot of snow. That would have created more problems with how to get it out of the water, where to keep it, and hope it can handle the harsh winter without any damage or other issues.

Sanford was able to get off work early that Friday, asked me to pack an overnight bag for him, and drive him to the airplane as soon as possible. He only had a few hours of daylight left to deliver the airplane, and it was going to be over a two-hour flight. We arrived at the airplane, and yes…Sanford took the time to recheck the fuel levels before takeoff. Trust but verify.

The flight went well, and Sanford successfully delivered the airplane. He had called ahead and they were on the river awaiting his arrival with a uniquely-designed truck and trailer to slide under the floats and pick the airplane out of the water. They drove it up a long ramp and to the airport where it would be housed for the winter. Sanford spent the night at friends' house and returned home Saturday morning on an early commercial flight. He was home before noon.

Sitting at home, enjoying a cup of coffee after breakfast, and while we watched the wind blow rain and sleet and snow outside, the phone rang. It was the owner of the Cessna. He knew Sanford expected to leave Saturday and was unhappy since the weather was so bad. He told Sanford he was just afraid he wouldn't have another chance to make the trip south. Plus he just wasn't sure what he was going to do with the airplane for the winter. Sanford told him the good news that it was already delivered, because looking at the weather on Friday he knew he had to leave then or not at all. The owner was in disbelief! Sanford explained what had happened the previous few days, and that he had already flown home on the airlines that morning.

Now that was one happy customer. Job well done.

Chapter 7

OATMEAL AND LAKE WATER

Living in Northern Minnesota was fantastic. It was hard work, year around, and we played hard, too. The weather was always a factor throughout the seasons as it brought different things to deal with. The winter brought extreme cold temperatures and lots of snow, so we had to do many things to prevent damage to the airplane and engine: Wing, tail, windshield, cowling, prop, and spinner covers put on to prevent frost, ice, and snow accumulation; pre-heat the engine before starting to help warm the oil and gauges; a good, strong battery to start in the cold; an insulated cover to keep the warmth in the engine when we stopped. The summer also brought extremes as well – wind, rain, and thunderstorms would pop up quickly; wide swings of temperatures; low and high lake levels creating new hazards or hiding the ones we already knew about; and the mosquitos…oh, the mosquitos!

We were planning to go camping on a summer weekend, so we went to our slip at the marina where we kept the airplane on floats on a Thursday evening. It was beautiful and calm, so we couldn't resist going for an evening flight before prepping our floatplane for the weekend trip. While on a quick flight around the area, we saw another floatplane as it was taxiing away from a municipal dock on the Canadian side of Rainy River that is used for clearing customs to enter Canada. We did not recognize the floatplane as anyone we knew. A few more minutes of flying before sunset, and we headed back to our slip.

After parking and securing our floatplane, we saw the same floatplane flying over us at the marina. We waved as he went by, thinking he was headed somewhere in Canada since we figured he had just cleared customs. A few minutes later, he has landed on the lake and is now taxiing into the marina, headed toward the shoreline alongside our floatplane. The pilot was alone in his floatplane, and got out to say hello. Sanford and I walked over to him and introduced ourselves. Sanford's standard introduction is: "Hi, my name is Sanford, like Sanford and Son, no son, just a cat." I like that because everyone, or at least those of us old enough to remember the television show, now understand what his first name is. I had never heard anyone else use a description to explain their first name, until what happened next. The pilot of the floatplane introduced himself, saying: "Hi, my name is Bernie, like the dead guy."

The look on Sanford's face! He was shocked at what Bernie had just said. I'm doubled-over laughing at both Sanford and Bernie! Obviously, Sanford did not understand what was so funny. I asked him if he had seen the movie, Weekend at Bernie's, and he said no. Now I'm laughing too hard again to explain to Sanford what the movie was about. Needless to say, we bought the movie and watched it the next weekend.

We asked Bernie if he needed some help. He said yes, that he wasn't sure where to go and camp for the night. He saw us flying and followed us to the marina, thinking we were local and could recommend a place. He had flown up that afternoon from a few hours away, and it was his first time in this area. He planned to fly around Canada and camp and do some fishing, and his floatplane was loaded down with lots of gear and barely had room for himself. Bernie had gotten delayed while clearing customs into Canada trying to find a Canadian aeronautical map, but none were available. Now he needed to find a place to camp for the night soon because the sun was setting and he did not know where to go. Luckily Sanford had an extra map in our floatplane and gave it to him.

Then Bernie noticed our U.S. registration number on our airplane and asked: "Oh, you keep your airplane in Canada when you're on floats?" Sanford told Bernie: "No, you're back in the United States. You shouldn't be here since you just cleared into Canada." Bernie was surprised, and obviously lost, and he had only just arrived. But dark was now setting in, and it was much too late for him to safely venture any distance in the floatplane. We told him of a campsite just a few minutes down the lake that would accommodate the floatplane, and recommended he get up early the next day and get back into Canada as soon as possible. We also explained to him where we would be camping over the weekend, but that it was too far up the lake for him to get there before dark.

Bernie agreed the closer campsite was a good idea. We exchanged contact information, wished him well and lots of fun, and invited Bernie to come back up sometime so we could go camping with the floatplanes together. We knew the area well and was looking forward to showing him some of our favorite spots.

Friday afternoon came, we loaded up our floatplane, and headed up the lake to a beautiful camping spot that had a small sand beach big enough to park and tie down the floatplane. It was not far from the campsite and made it easy to carry our gear back and forth. So much so we always brought enough gear and supplies to be comfortable. We were going to camp for two nights and always brought some extra food, just in case.

Saturday morning, we were in our small boat, fishing off our favorite reef just a few hundred yards out from the campsite. We hear an airplane. We see a floatplane. It's Bernie. Seems he had tried to find a place to camp and fish in the closer lakes in Canada, and didn't have any luck. Either the shorelines were filled with rocks or trees right to the edge so he could not park his floatplane, or when the shoreline was clear it contained a cabin and dock and appeared to be private property. He decided to clear back into the U.S. and come find us.

We moved our floatplane to the side enough that Bernie could park his alongside on the beach. We helped him carry his gear up to camp, and he quickly pitched his tent and settled in. We invited Bernie to go with us for a boat ride to one of our favorite places. The three of us climbed in our 12-foot boat and headed through the channels to one of the prettiest spots on Rainy Lake called Kettle Falls Hotel. It was built around the year 1900 by a madame to service the loggers and trappers in the area. It is accessible only by boat, airplane, or snowmobile, and is now owned by the U.S. National Park Service. The building has been restored back to its original state, using all the original lumber, and is a full-service hotel, bar, and restaurant. Back in the day, it was a full-service hotel as well…of a different kind. If those walls could talk…

Bernie had no idea where we were going and was amazed when we came upon the hotel. We walked up and ordered lunch and something to drink. Bernie was quick to down a couple of ice-cold beers, which he thought was quite a treat for his weekend of remote, bring-only-the-bare-necessities flying, fishing, and camping. In fact, when Bernie arrived in his floatplane, he was wearing chest waders with tennis shoes large enough to go over the waders. He thought he would be maneuvering the floatplane in the water a lot, so he dressed for the occasion.

And since space was precious in his floatplane, he did not bring any other shoes. When we invited him for the boat ride, we told him he would not need his waders. He left them at camp, put on his oversized tennis shoes, and climbed in the boat. I think they were about three sizes too big and looked like long, wide clown shoes without the waders. We had a wonderful meal, and headed back to camp.

Saturday night supper was always worth looking forward to. We had our standard items on the menu – the best T-bone steaks we could find, baked potatoes wrapped in foil and thrown right in the coals of the campfire, baked beans, fire-toasted garlic toast, and cocktails with ice cubes, of course. There is nothing like a good steak cooked over a campfire. Bernie had made sandwiches before his trip, and insisted he was just fine. We did have an extra potato and baked beans, and immediately said yes when Sanford offered it to him. Bernie also let us know that he just happened to like the same kind of brandy that Sanford was drinking. We had an extra cup, some ice, and Bernie was grinning from ear to ear. A great campfire, great food, good conversation, a couple of cocktails, and it was time to say goodnight.

We are early risers and were up with the sun the next morning. In the summer, sunrise occurs around 5:00 am in Northern Minnesota. We never wanted to miss a moment of daylight. We made coffee over the campfire, and Sanford was already preparing breakfast. Of course, we had our standard items on the menu: Eggs, bacon, hash browns, and toast with butter. Bernie woke up to the smell of coffee and came out of his tent with the cup he had used for cocktails the night before. Sanford pulled the coffee pot off the fire and poured us all a cup.

Bernie noticed Sanford was preparing breakfast, so he headed back to his tent and returned with his breakfast gear. He had a single-burner cookstove, a small aluminum pan, a spoon, his coffee, and a couple packets of instant oatmeal. He sat down at the picnic table and asked what we were having for breakfast. Sanford told him what was on the menu, and we asked what he was having. Bernie replied, in the most sorrowful and forlorn tone, sadly looking at the ground: "Oatmeal and lake water." Trying not to laugh out loud, we invited Bernie to have breakfast with us. Without saying a word, Bernie sprang from the picnic table, carrying his cookstove, pan, spoon, and oatmeal, and ran back to the tent. He returned in the same fashion, hands empty – all while wearing those three-sizes-too-big tennis shoes, and said an excited: "Sure!" As you know, we always bring extra.

We stayed in touch with Bernie, and he returned later that summer to camp with us again and brought his father along. Bernie had told him about his adventure to Northern Minnesota and wanted to share it with his dad. Bernie flew his floatplane up again, but it was loaded so full with camping gear his dad had to drive. They left about the same time, and arrived about the same time. Bernie made two trips from our slip at the marina to the campsite. One to bring his dad up and the second to bring his gear. Another memorable time with good friends and fun airplanes.

This time Bernie's shoes fit much better.

Chapter 8

Rainy Lake Rescues

We lived in International Falls, Minnesota, for nearly 18 years and enjoyed all aspects the outdoors had to offer. Boating, flying, float flying, ski flying, snowmobiling, hunting, camping, fishing, and of course, ice fishing. One of our favorite traditions was to go fishing on Christmas Day and land on the frozen lake with the airplane on wheels, drill some holes in the ice, fish until we got our limit, and head home for a meal of fresh fish. But of all these combined, the float flying was the most spectacular.

Sanford constantly practiced techniques with the airplane to make sure he was ready for any situation. He told me many times he needed to know exactly what the airplane could do, and could not do. He would practice high-speed taxi techniques on the water. And he would practice landing techniques on smooth, glassy water since it created no depth perception for landing.

Glassy water landings are one of the most dangerous. If you think you can judge your touchdown on glassy water, you would most likely be wrong. Many people think they are about to touch down when they are actually still several feet above the water. This can cause a severe series of accelerated bounces, called porpoising, and loss of control of the floatplane, doing major damage to the float structure, or worse, flipping the floatplane upside down in the water. This obviously has a devastating end.

Sanford tells pilots to get to know their aircraft. On our Cessna 170, the proper numbers for a safe glassy water landing are: Descend over the trees as low as possible down to the water; reduce power to 1,950 rpm, add 20° of flaps, and pitch the nose up so the floatplane will maintain a 50 mph airspeed. This creates a descend rate of approximately 200 feet per minute. Once you get into ground effect close to the water, it will automatically reduce your rate of descent to about 20 feet per minute, creating a safe, slow descend onto the water. When you feel touchdown, do not assume you are on the water. Make sure you visually see the water spray coming from the sides of the floats. Sometimes you will feel an air current that feels the same as touching down on the water. Many people will relax and assume they have landed, but instead still have ten feet or so to go. This puts a whole new meaning to the term 'splash down'. This is the only safe technique for landing on glassy water.

Sanford would also practice landing on wheels at the main airport, putting one wheel down on the center line of the runway and drive it all the way to the end. He would then come around and put the other wheel down, doing it again. Flying is very instinctive and natural for Sanford, and his instincts serve him well.

Sanford and I were well known in the community, and Sanford especially for his flying. We were occasionally asked to help someone, from finding lost cattle or horses, to taking photos of property lines for legal issues. We helped with search and rescue missions when a hunter or boater was overdue returning home. We also helped with getting injured people to medical help, bringing them in from the remote wilderness of Northern Minnesota.

One winter brought the usual amount of snow and good, cold weather to provide enough ice on the lakes to safely support cars and trucks and snowmobiles. And airplanes. We fitted our Cessna with skis each winter and enjoyed the cold, crisp sunny days that brought the bluest skies you have ever seen and sparkling snow. Some days the temperature never got above zero, but the sun would still provide some warmth. The cold air provided added performance for the airplane, making it fun and easy to fly.

We headed to one of our favorite resorts for lunch on a Sunday afternoon. Many snowmobilers also gathered at the resorts throughout the area. It was very social and fun to meet people from the immediate area and all over the country enjoying their vacations. We were just about to depart and head for home when someone asked if that was our airplane.

Sanford said yes and asked why. Some snowmobilers had called the resort to report they were bringing in a friend who had an accident with his snowmobile and was injured. We did not know what type of injury, but they said he would need to get to a hospital right away. The snowmobilers were not from the area and needed help finding transportation as well as a hospital. They asked if Sanford could help, and he said yes.

The snowmobilers arrived shortly with their injured friend. Their best guess was a broken collar bone or broken arm. With the injury and long, rough ride back to the resort on the snowmobile, the injured man was not doing well and in tremendous pain. We were afraid shock was setting in. Sanford loaded the injured man into the back seat of the airplane so he could sit somewhat sideways to help him be more comfortable. The flight went smoothly, and Sanford got him to the nearest hospital for medical attention. The flight was far less than half the time it would have taken to drive.

One summer, we had gone in with several other friends and rented a houseboat for the weekend. Most of the friends rode on the houseboat and found a nice sandy beach about 20 miles east of town. It was in a channel, protected from the majority of the wind, and would be a fun place to spend the weekend. We arrived in our Cessna on floats and parked the airplane on the beach next to the houseboat. The weather was a perfect summer day and the water was warm enough to swim.

In the afternoon, Sanford took one of our friends for a floatplane ride. While he was gone, another friend arrived by boat to say hello. We had left the marine-band radio on in the houseboat and was casually listening to other houseboats as they navigated the lake and islands. Then we heard several calls from one particular houseboat to the main base where they had rented it. No one answered. The calls got more frantic and soon they were calling for anyone on the lake. Someone had gotten injured and needed to get to a hospital.

I had a hand-held aircraft radio and tried to get hold of Sanford. I thought he should be on his way back, but with the limited distance the radio provided, he could not hear me. Our friend driving the boat knew the lake well and offered to help. They described their location and found it was not far from us. I rode along in the boat to help and to keep hailing Sanford on the aircraft radio. When we arrived at the houseboat, we found that another boater had also heard their pleas for help and drove over. But he was not from the area and did not know the lake. It was vast and full of islands and rocks. If you strayed away from the channel, which is quite narrow at times, you stood a good chance of wrecking your boat.

The other boater already had the injured lady and her husband loaded in his boat. They appeared to be near retirement age, and they were on vacation with their family from Indiana. It was their first time on Rainy Lake. She had walked out to the edge of the lake as evening was starting to set in to watch the last of the sun on the water. She slipped, fell on the large, jagged rocks, broke her forearm and slashed her knees. She was in tremendous pain and bleeding and very scared. Since the other boater did not know the way, we decided to have him follow us to town rather than try to move her to another boat. We gave the other boater strict instructions to stay in our wake at all times to avoid hitting reefs and rocks, especially through the narrows. I was still trying to hail Sanford on the aircraft radio when we departed for town, which was more than an hour away.

Shortly after we departed, I heard Sanford on the radio. He had heard me and was on his way to find us. I told him our location with the two boats, and he was just a couple minutes behind. We decided to move the injured lady to the floatplane and fly her to town to the hospital. Now we needed to get her out of the boat and into the floatplane. That part went well. It was getting the other boater to stop because he was confused as to why. We told him we were going to take her the rest of the way in an airplane. He said what airplane, and we said turn around, just as Sanford landed behind us. We needed to maneuver the floatplane alongside the boats for the transfer of both the injured lady and myself. With three of us in the floatplane, however, her husband would not fit and he needed a boat ride to town. Our friend said he would, and we sent the other boater back to his houseboat before it got too dark.

Considering what this poor lady had already been through, she was doing quite well and was very calm. This was her first airplane ride and was sorry it was under such circumstances. They had wrapped her in a jacket and comforter, and had bandaged her knees as best they could. She had trouble moving her legs, so we put her in the back seat sort of sideways to keep her as comfortable as possible. During the flight to town, Sanford radioed the airport and advised we had an injured person aboard who needed immediate medical attention. The airport called the ambulance and had them meet us on the river near town, just a half mile away from the hospital. We landed in the river just as the ambulance and police arrived at the boat landing. With their help, the lady was gently moved from the airplane to the ambulance. Her injuries were substantial, but she recovered well over the next several weeks at home. I'm sure this is a vacation she will never forget.

Now Sanford and I are on the river in town and need to return to the houseboat, some 25 miles east. And it was after dark – not a good place to be in a floatplane on the water. Since Sanford knew the bay well where the houseboat was parked, plus he had honed his glassy water landing technique, we felt confident it would be no problem to fly back and enjoy the rest of the weekend. The Cessna has a landing light in the wing that would help illuminate the water and area around us.

As we came in over the trees to the bay, Sanford was getting the floatplane set for the landing. Low approach over the trees, rpm's, flaps, and nose-high attitude to maintain his landing speed. Flip on the landing light, and poof! Both bulbs burned out! Sanford did not flinch, knowing he was set up perfectly for a safe landing. And a safe and smooth landing he did. Practice makes perfect, and the landing technique worked again.

We had a beautiful winter one year that provided good snow, lots of ice, no slush, and abundant sunshine. We had the airplane on skis, and enjoyed more than the usual amount of flying on the nice weekends. One Saturday afternoon, while we were on the way back to the airport after a full day of flying, we saw a single snowmobile on the lake trail with the hood up. We could see several miles in the distance and could see someone walking toward town, but could not see any other snowmobiles in sight. It was late in the afternoon, just before the sun went down, it was already cold, and quickly getting colder. We were at least ten miles from town and knew the driver would not be able to walk the entire way.

We flew up to the driver and got his attention, and he started waving with both arms. Sanford brought the airplane in and landed just behind him, and asked if he needed help. He said his snowmobile broke down, and the group he was riding with had not stopped to help. And knowing it was getting dark soon, he thought he had better start walking. The driver was not from the area, and really had no idea how far he was from civilization. We offered him a ride in the airplane to town so he could catch up with his group, and he gladly accepted. He had obviously been drinking quite a bit that day, so needless to say his judgement was quite impaired.

We loaded the driver into the back seat of the airplane and took off for town. He told us where his group had planned to stop next, which was a restaurant and bar along the lake, and was very popular with snowmobilers. Sanford landed the airplane near the shore where all the snowmobiles were parked and dropped off our passenger. Even more grateful now that he knew he would not have made it, the driver offered to pay us for the airplane ride. We declined, of course, and when we landed at the airport, we found a $20 bill in the back seat. I think he wanted to buy us a drink! The driver was excited to rejoin his friends in the bar and tell them his story about the airplane.

Most likely the other snowmobilers did not believe him, at least until the next day when they retrieved the snowmobile and could see the tracks of the airplane in the snow. My inclination was to recommend to the driver that he should look for another group to ride with since they apparently did not know he was missing until he walked into the bar.

Sanford had been flying floats for several summers now and was very proficient. He continued to practice different landing and takeoff techniques for use in different situations, and that practice paid off.

We decided to camp one weekend over Labor Day. It was a long weekend for both of us from work, and the weather was beautiful. It was the end of summer in Northern Minnesota, so we wanted to enjoy it as much as possible. We had gotten an early start on Friday afternoon, loaded the floatplane, and flew up to one of our favorite camping spots about 20 miles east on Rainy Lake from town.

Earlier in the week I had seen the dentist and had a root canal done on one of my front upper teeth. My follow up appointment had been on Thursday, and all looked good so the dentist gave me the green light to take off for the weekend. I was excited and feeling good on Friday and ready for a weekend with Sanford.

Sometime on Saturday afternoon I realized I had a toothache, and it was the tooth with the fresh root canal. I took some aspirin to help ease the ache and decided to ignore it. A couple hours later I couldn't, and got myself an ice pack. That seemed to dull the ache again for a while, but not for long. It is evening now and this thing is in a full roar. I can feel a growing bump on my gum under my lip, and I realize I am not going to be able to stand it much longer. It was well after dark now. Sanford decided to try and call the dentist even though it was a holiday weekend. The island had little to no cell phone service, but he found one rock that provided one bar of service. The after-hours answering service gave Sanford the dentist's home phone number, but he was not at home. His daughter answered and advised he was at their family cabin on the lake and gave Sanford her father's cell phone number.

Sanford got hold of the dentist and described my situation. The dentist advised it was an abscess caused by infection that was still present when they sealed the tooth. Since it was a front tooth, it was near the sinuses, and if it burst, it would send the poison directly to my brain, which was deadly. Sanford needed to get me to the hospital as soon as possible to drain the abscess by either lancing it or drilling out the tooth.

It is now well after midnight, and we are in the wilderness with only the floatplane as transportation. My condition could not wait as time was of the essence since the abscess was constantly growing in size. It was completely dark and navigating the lake back to town was not going to be easy. But that's when all his practice and training with landings and takeoffs in different conditions came into play. Sanford knew the lake well, and already had his landing site picked out in his head before we took off. He knew where the channel markers were and where he needed to be to navigate around the rocks. This year was especially challenging since the lake level was extremely low, making new obstacles of rocks that were not a problem under normal conditions.

I don't remember much of the flight, but I do remember his landing on the eerie, black water on the lake. It looked completely foreign to me, but Sanford knew exactly where we were to the inch. He set up for landing, and I could begin to make out the tops of the trees. We cleared the trees with an open channel of the lake in front of us. He set the power, added some flaps, and held the nose of the floatplane up slightly to maintain a certain speed, and waited. Patience is a virtue. Sanford had the floatplane in a slight descent and was waiting for the water to come up and meet us. Since he could not tell exactly where the water was, this made sure we would not flare too high and stall the floatplane. Wait, wait, and then we gently glided onto the surface of the water. I remember Sanford power-taxiing to the dock to park the floatplane and get our pickup. Normally he coasts up to a dock, coming in slow and gentle. But with the low water, we had stopped in the muck on the bottom, much too far from the dock to reach it. At nearly full power, Sanford moved the rudders on the airplane tail section and floats back and forth to their maximum, sort of wagging the tail. This way he maneuvered the floatplane close enough to jump to the dock, and was able to pull it the rest of the way in. We secured the floatplane, jumped in the pickup, and off to the hospital.

I will admit I was not a good patient in the emergency room, growing more and more irritated with the pain. The ice no longer helped, and the doctor wanted to try a couple of things, like pain medications and Novocain, to dull it. After over an hour and four shots of different medications, the pain had not subsided. I was plenty irritated now and not in the mood to delay it any longer. I insisted the doctor just lance and drain it to get it over with, and he finally agreed. It was over in a few seconds and the pressure was finally gone. The pain remained, and I was still plenty irritated, but we could finally go home around 3:00 am.

Strange enough I felt good the next morning with the aching pain finally gone, and got up early since I couldn't sleep. I took a long, hot shower which felt good, and went to the kitchen to make some coffee and let Sanford sleep. I poured a cup of coffee and went to sit down and catch up on the computer. It was then that my adrenaline finally subsided and all four pain medication shots took hold. I barely made it back to bed and slept the next twelve hours.

Sanford saved my life that night. And he has most likely saved the lives of many of the other people he has helped over the years, using his talent and skill and knowledge of flying an airplane. We both feel fortunate to be able use our equipment and his skills to help people, especially at times like these. We are truly blessed.

Chapter 9

The Last Frontier

From Sanford's collection:

The U.S. Department of Interior, located in the great state of Alaska, had a fleet of small aging aircraft called Piper Super Cubs. They had been the work horses needed to travel in and around one of the most extreme and remote parts of the world. To this day, the Super Cub is highly coveted, and is the best-known aircraft for reliability and performance, having the ability to get in and out of small areas. Plus, they are capable of handling just about everything Alaska's weather has in its four seasons. With the right experience, a pilot has the ability to handle some fairly strong winter winds. The visibility in the front seat of a Super Cub is superior to other airplanes. It is great for spotting things, from people on the ground, to fish in the ocean. The Super Cub can easily be rigged with floats for landing on water, as well as skis for the snow. They can be rigged with large, soft bush tires for short landing capability in places like river gravel bars, the frozen tundra, or the shoreline along the ocean. The Cub can haul all sorts of cargo, things like medical supplies, mail, or doctors and medicine to very remote parts of the country that had been accessible in the winter only by dog sleds. Fishing and hunting in Alaska is also a very important part of survival. For most of us, we simply go to the corner store and buy groceries to cook dinner. But that's just not the case in this remote and self-reliant part of the world. Some of the best food in the world lives in the beautiful waters and the vast natural wilderness of Alaska. Some of these places are only accessible from an aircraft of this type. A very important part of the Alaska life style is to maintain hunting and fishing forever. This is the responsibility of the U.S. Department of Interior, to manage these precious resources.

The old fleet of Super Cubs had been rebuilt many times and were tired and overworked. The fleet needed to be updated with brand new airplanes. The government purchased several new Top Cubs for their new fleet. The airplanes were built in Washington State, and now it was up to me to deliver them.

Flying to Alaska is not a walk in the park. My first delivery was going to be in February, smack-dab in the middle of the harshest part of winter. Very, very few people even consider flying that time of the year, let alone all the way to Alaska through Canada and the Yukon, especially in a small single-engine aircraft. If anything went wrong, it could be a death sentence for sure. My many years of experience flying in Northern Minnesota and Canada were going to be extremely valuable. I flew year around, in all kinds of weather, and temperatures down as low as 33° below Fahrenheit. Planning and preparing for survivability in those temperatures is mandatory. I always flew with survival gear, including several ways of starting a fire. Most unintentional off-airport landings are very survivable. However, you are almost always guaranteed that you will be spending the first night out in the wilderness by yourself. The biggest and deadliest problem is to survive hypothermia when the freezing temperatures can get in the extremes.

I have experienced hypothermia, and let me tell you, it's not like you think. I have seen grown men get lost while hunting, try to find their way back, and cross a highway and never realize it. When they were finally found, they had actually removed their winter clothing before they died. Many have been found close to civilization, but were unable to get help or shelter because their mind did not function correctly. I was asked one time, what does it feel like to be exposed to 40° below temperatures. I replied, you don't feel cold, you feel pain!

One of the fire starters I carry in my survival gear are cotton balls saturated with petroleum jelly in a sealable bag. When you need to build a fire, simply take one of the cotton balls and form it into something that looks like a little Hershey kiss with a candle wick on top. Each cotton ball will burn for approximately eight minutes. Even wet wood, such as twigs and branches, are dry inside. Have a knife or small axe to make small kindling that will light and burn easily. If it is still daylight, and you are physically able, gather as much wood as you can until the sun goes down. Once it is dark, the wood store closes for the day! I tell pilots to make a big fire. Big fires give you courage! You will need courage to stay warm and survive the night. After all, this will probably be one of the scariest nights a pilot will ever face!

I also carry a roll of duct tape in my survival kit. This can be useful in so many different ways, from building a shelter, making a splint for a broken limb, or even closing a wound to keep from bleeding to death. Chances are, you will not be in the wilderness long enough to think about getting hungry. But there are a few things that would be good to have, such as a nice dry roll of toilet paper! Mosquito repellent is almost a necessity to have in the summertime, and have a way to melt snow or purify swamp water for drinking.

Flight planning for my first Alaska trip was going to be extensive to say the least. First thing I needed to do was plan the route, so paper aviation charts were ordered and spread out in my living room. There were so many, it filled the entire floor. With safety and survivability as my first priority, I plotted several courses to minimize the danger. A large portion of the trip would take me through the Rocky Mountains, and I needed to find a route that would keep me as low as possible. As luck would have it, somebody already figured that out. It's called highways! Rivers also find their way through the mountains in the lowest possible places. I just had to find a road or a river going my way.

For the first few trips in the winter, I decided to stay close to the Alaskan highway. That way if I had to, I could land on the highway and hopefully be found easily. Finding fuel stops would also be important. Back in the 1940's, the government built a road and airports through Canada and the Yukon to Alaska, just in case Alaska was invaded. I called and documented each and every airport to find out if they had fuel, tie downs, hangars, and electrical plug-ins for the heater in the engine. I quickly found out hangars were not available, anywhere. Tie downs were also not available, since the snow plows cover up the tie-down anchors with ice and snow. I needed to acquire covers for the wings, tail, and windshield to keep off the frost and snow. I needed at least 100 feet of extension cord to plug in the heater, and an engine blanket to hold in the warmth. I also needed an alternate way to warm up the engine with no electricity, in case I was forced to make an off-airport landing. I needed to calculate flying time and distance between fuel stops to make sure I was able to arrive at an airport or town or motel while it was still daylight, which at that time of the year is very short. Another thing to consider is cell phones do not work in the wilderness.

I documented everything and compiled as much information as possible. I also had to brush up on Canadian aviation regulations, though similar to the U.S., there are some things that are done differently. The requirements for flying through the wilderness in Canada are more stringent when it comes to filing flight plans. During my trips, I found

Canadian flight service to be extremely helpful. Clearing customs would be necessary for going into Canada, as well as returning into the U.S. in Alaska. Flying in Northern Minnesota, I was very used to clearing Canada and U.S. customs, so that was easy for me.

I know I am not the first pilot to make this trip. However, I didn't know anyone that I could ask questions and take advice from. And then I met Marv – Marvelous Marv! He is a retired gentleman that, as a teenager, grew up living on the side of a mountain in a small camper all by himself, except for his cat, named Otamar P. Snyder. As a kitten in the winter, Marv would take Otamar along inside his jacket, worried that he would not survive the cold alone at the camper. Marv said: "Don't know how to spell it. The cat was named after a 1954 Winter Olympics downhill ski champion by a school bus load of Highland High School girls at White Pass ski hill. Never looked it up. Didn't care. But old Oty attracted girls. I mean, who knew! Who cared! I'm 18 and learning."

Marv's small camper was located in the mountains at the end of the main road. He is the type of man that has a very unique ability to survive and fix anything. While a young man still in school, he needed to find a job, and a way to get to school and stay in school. He talked to the principal and got a job driving the school bus. At the end of the school day, he would drive the bus home, dropping off his classmates along the way. Then the next morning he would drive the bus down the mountain back to school, picking up his classmates. A unique man to say the least!

After graduating high school, Marv first joined the Marines for four years. After a four-year break, he joined the Navy for five years, working in two different submarines as a mechanic. He has a great mechanical background and spent much of his life in Alaska working as an industrial machine mechanic on the Alaskan highway and the Alaskan pipeline, to say nothing about the North Slope. Marv is no stranger to cold and adverse weather conditions. He told me he has driven the Alaskan highway 18 times during his career in Alaska. Some mornings he would get up from sleeping in the back of his pickup to make oatmeal on the tailgate and watched as an airplane flew past. As a pilot, he has always wished that someday he would be able to fly his own airplane to Alaska.

I did my best to convince Marv into coming along with me, and he jumped at the opportunity! There were two brand-new airplanes ready to go, and all I had to do was give him a quick check out. I found Marv to be an excellent pilot, and I was lucky to have him as my wingman. Marv is as close to a mentor as I will ever find!

Marv designed and manufactured two identical heaters that we could use to preheat the engines of the aircraft without electrical power. They were designed to run on the high-octane fuel used in the airplanes. And since we were already carrying fuel in the wing tanks, we could simply siphon some out to fire up the heaters. All of our survival gear had to fit in the airplanes, and the heaters were very compact since space was limited. Plus, all the gear had to come back with us on the airlines to be used again on the next aircraft deliveries.

More than a month of planning was now complete, and it was time to head north. I was happy Marv was coming along with me because flying to Alaska is very dangerous this time of year, and something I did not want to face alone. I knew this was definitely going to be a trip of a lifetime. We arrived early in the morning, said our goodbyes, and set out on a journey that was bigger than life. We filed flight plans, called Canadian customs, and departed for the last great frontier. Our first stop was 3-1/2 hours later, and we landed in Kamloops, British Columbia, Canada, to clear customs and get fuel. While heading north on the very first leg of the trip, things went south rapidly!

The plane that my good friend Marv was flying had a major brake failure. The day before we left, one of the mechanics at the factory decided the brake system needed more fluid. That turned out to be a bad decision. As a result of over-filling the system, both brakes were locked up on landing, causing a very dangerous and possibly fatal situation. But with Marv's skill, he did not get hurt and was able to save the airplane. In the process, the propeller and engine were damaged and both had to be replaced. My friend would have to wait a few more weeks before continuing on the trip and completing his dream. As his commercial flight home was ready to take off and head south, I departed the airport and continued north, hoping he didn't see me leave without him.

Now I was on my own! It was the first part of February, and the worst time to be flying to Alaska. As the rest of the trip turned out for me, it might have been a good thing that he was not able to go any further.

I departed Kamloops and climbed up over the mountains, and plotted a course for my next stops at Prince George and then Fort Nelson, British Columbia. The further north I flew, the more winter it got. The temperature continued to drop, and I could see there was more snow on the ground. I contacted the airport control tower at Fort Nelson and landed just before dark. Daylight hours are very short and the first thing was to secure the airplane. There were no hangars in Fort Nelson for airplanes since all the buildings were full with helicopters. The main industry in the area is gas wells, and the helicopters are used to fly the maintenance people to and from the wells.

There was about six inches of fresh snow on the ground and no tie downs. I brought 100 feet of extension cord along and found a place to plug in the engine heater. I put on the wing, tail, windshield, and cowling covers in the dark. Once the aircraft was secure for the night, I had to find lodging and transportation to a hotel. In that part of the country, there is no sense of urgency when it comes to taxi service. Turns out there was only one taxi in town, so I made a reservation for the next morning to be back at the airport early before sunrise. The next day's weather forecast ahead of me did not look good. The aviation weather forecast is for what might happen at airports. But there can be 300 to 400 miles between airports, all mountainous terrain, and the mountains make their own weather. As I readied the aircraft in the morning darkness, I noticed that four more inches of snow fell during the night, and it had a crunchy sound as I walked around the airplane. That only happens when it's below zero!

The sun finally came up to a cloudy day, but the weather was improving. I departed to the west for Watson Lake in the Yukon Territory. The plan was to follow the Alaskan highway, but low, patchy clouds blocked the mountain passes. I found a beautiful hole in the clouds and got on top to look up ahead. It was like heaven! The sunny bright blue skies made the mountains look pure and untouched with the fresh snow that fell during the night. The top of the mountains had a hard, frosty crust that I have never seen before, almost like from another planet. I was thinking how lucky I was to see this. Then I realized I had no one to share it with. It also made me realize where I was and how completely I was on my own. There is no 9-1-1 here. No help could ever come if there was a problem. They wouldn't even know where to look. No time to make any mistakes, and it was time to press on.

As the sun finally melted the clouds away, I returned to following the ice-covered highway. Miles and miles of road and I never saw any cars or trucks. Up near the Liard River I saw something on the road, so I went down to take a look. I couldn't believe my eyes. An entire herd of bison were laying in the middle of the road. What a surprise to see them on the road, but why not since there was no traffic. I'm thinking they stayed on the road so they could defend themselves from timber wolves. If the wolves could chase them off the road and push them out into the deep snow, the wolf pack could attack. No predator is going to get close to these big guys in the middle of the road and live!

Another hour down the road and I arrived at Watson Lake for fuel. This was another airport built because of the cold war. It had a huge wooden control tower in the terminal building that was closed to the public because of its age and structural safety concerns. The terminal looks like the last person left ten minutes ago, but it hasn't been used in many, many years. Black-and-white photos of yester-year war planes and pilots hung on the walls. They tell the stories of the pilots flying the bombers and fighter planes through the area to deliver them to Russia. Some of the photos were of airplanes that met their demise while flying through this unforgiving wilderness.

Next stop, Whitehorse in the Yukon Territory. I arrived just before dark and found a place to park close enough to a building that I could plug in the airplane's engine heater. By the time I pulled the wing covers out of the airplane, it was already dark. After securing the aircraft I searched for a hotel and transportation to town. Here again, Whitehorse was built back in the 1940's in case war broke out. The military barracks are now converted to hotels and housing. At the airport entrance is a full-size DC-3 airplane mounted on a pedestal that serves as a weathervane. Amazingly, it only takes about 2 mph to turn it into the wind. Once I finally got to the hotel in town, I felt like I stepped back in history. Nothing has changed, the buildings, the furniture, they are all the same as if time stood still since World War II.

Thousands of people with gold fever traveled through this town over the years, hoping to discover gold and strike it rich. This is where the Yukon River starts. Near the frozen river bank is a huge river boat with a paddle wheel that is now a museum. On one of my next trips to Alaska, I had an opportunity to go on a private tour during the summer. Not much luxury aboard since the boats were mainly used to carry supplies up and down the river. They were hard times!

I returned to the airport early the next morning before daybreak. I repeated the process of removing and storing the wing covers, tail covers, windshield covers, engine blanket, and extension cord. Again, the snow had a crunch underneath my feet. The temperature was well below zero, and my fingers and toes already hurt. I started the engine and took off just as the sun was starting to come up. Next stop was Northway, Alaska, to clear customs back into the U.S. The customs officers have to drive from the Alaskan border-crossing along the highway to the Northway airport, which takes about an hour. I needed to arrive plus or minus ten minutes of my appointment time to clear customs. The airport was completely abandoned and no fuel was available, but the runway was plowed. It looked like about four inches of solid, compacted ice on the runway. Just as I landed, the customs officer arrived at the airport. I stayed in the airplane until they walked over to me, and then circled around the airplane with a Geiger counter. They must worry that someone might bring a nuclear bomb into the country in such a tiny airplane!

With the winter winds and extremely cold temperatures, it did not take customs very long to clear me back into the States. The officer was back in his warm truck, and I was back in the air within a couple of minutes. Then it was a quick 30-minute flight, and I landed in Tok, Alaska. In total it had been a four-hour flight to Tok, and I needed more fuel. It was also good to see civilization again.

As I departed, I turned west toward Anchorage, it started to snow, and the winds started to rage. I was quickly in a full-blown Alaskan winter storm. The mountains were making their own weather, and the turbulence was unimaginable. My little airplane was showing that I was doing 100 mph, but my ground speed was reading only 20 mph. Yes, 80 mph winds in the mountains created some of the worst turbulence I have ever experienced. I was concerned I would have structural failure in the airplane. I was violently tossed around in the cockpit, knocking off my headset, and all the loose objects thrown around. I had to reach into my bag of tricks before something went terribly wrong. I pulled back on the control stick and slowed the airplane down, as if I were driving a boat in high waves, in a nose-high attitude, slowly mushing through instead of taking hard hits, so as not to do any damage. Watching ahead of me I could see bursts of snow from the ground shooting high up into the air. The wind was coming down over the mountain tops so hard and violently, that when it hit the ground, it made the snow explode straight up like a huge water spout. Then the swirling wind made them look like snow tornadoes. With no airports around, I had to figure out how to survive. I knew the Alaskan highway was just a few miles away, so I slowly fought my way over to it. Once I was over the road, I dropped down below the tree tops and flew as close to the highway as I could – about two feet over it. I remember looking up at the tops of the trees as the 80 mph wind was bending the trees over, but it could not reach me. With no traffic on the highway because of winter, I was able to follow it for many miles. I finally flew out of the storm and arrived in Anchorage.

I was glad my friend Marv was back home safe. That was the worst storm I have ever experienced in my life.

On my third trip to Alaska, the second airplane was now repaired and Marv was able to complete his trip of a lifetime. We had the most beautiful weather I've ever seen in my life. The mountains appeared to smile on me once again.

Chapter 10

Marv's Journey

After Marv had the brake failure with the Top Cub in Kamloops, British Columbia, Canada, he flew home on a commercial flight while Sanford proceeded north in the other Top Cub. The repairs to the airplane were going to be done right there in Kamloops, but they would take several weeks to complete. Once finished, Marv planned to fly with Sanford in another brand-new Top Cub to be delivered to Anchorage, and pick up the repaired airplane along the way.

In recalling his first flight to the Kamloops airport, where the brakes were locked up on landing, Marv remembers it all happened so suddenly that he did not know what was going on. But with his skill and instinct and experience as a pilot, Marv was able to keep the airplane from flipping over and injuring, or worse yet, killing him. He kept the damage on the airplane to just the engine and propeller, but it was still a mystery at the time of what just happened.

Then Marv told me about seeing that Top Cub just before he and Sanford would leave on their first flight. Marv was at his hangar at the

Yakima airport, preparing his gear for the first flight, and said he heard an airplane taxi by. Normally, that would just be regular traffic and not that notable. But this time it was, because he could hear a loud, high-pitch squeal, as well as the engine running at higher-than-normal rpm's. He stepped outside to see what was going on, only to discover it was the Top Cub being taxied past by a pilot/mechanic for storage in a nearby hangar. It was unusual and he wondered why the pilot did not stop to investigate the problem. The airplane continued on, and Marv continued with his careful preparation, dismissing the incident at the time.

Now looking back, Marv and Sanford both realized the pilot taxiing the airplane was the mechanic that had made a last-minute adjustment to the brakes. In the short distance the mechanic had taxied the airplane that day, the brakes were already showing signs of locking up, causing the loud squeal and requiring much more power even to just taxi on the ground.

Departure morning arrived for Marv's second trip. Since the damaged airplane was now repaired and ready to go, Marv and Sanford rode together in another brand-new Top Cub from Yakima to Kamloops. They planned to pick it up and continue on to Anchorage as a flight of two. With Marv in the front seat and Sanford in the back, they had a second chance to complete the journey together.

They are on final and set for landing at the Kamloops airport. The weather was clear and the surface of the runway was dry. It was still winter, and there was still significant snow on the ground. As Marv touched down for landing, both brakes failed in the new Top Cub! But Sanford was ready for it this time, and took control of the airplane. Sanford was able to keep it from flipping over and from striking the propeller on the ground. After gaining control and coming to a complete stop on the runway, the brakes are now completely locked up and they cannot move. Sanford radioed the control tower to advise they could not taxi the airplane because of the brake failure. They were cleared to stay on the runway until the brakes would release. After several minutes, the brakes started to release and they taxied to the parking area on the ramp, needing a lot of power because the brakes were still binding. After shutting down the airplane, they decided to remove some of the brake fluid to release the pressure. With wrench in hand, Sanford loosened the nut to the brake line, expecting the fluid to slowly drain out. Instead, the fluid was under so much pressure, it spouted out and shot straight up in the air. After doing some checking back at the Cub Crafters factory, it was confirmed that the same mechanic had made an adjustment to the brakes the night before on this new airplane as well.

Sanford and Marv now needed to check the repaired airplane to see if the brakes are still a problem. They both got in the airplane and taxied it around the airport, expecting the brakes to lock up again in a short period of time. And they did. Now this airplane cannot move until the brakes release. Wrench in hand, they repeated the process of draining brake fluid, with the same result of it spouting out and shooting straight up in the air. Now they both know for certain what happened to Marv on that first landing.

After clearing Canadian customs, dealing with the brake failures on both airplanes, fueling both airplanes, and sorting and transferring gear, it was too late in the day to fly another leg of the trip to their next stop at Prince George. They decided to spend the night in Kamloops, get some rest, and start fresh the next day. With Marv up early, packed, and ready to go the following morning, Sanford asked him where he was going. They woke up to low ceilings and poor visibility, delaying their departure yet another day. The pilots enjoyed a good breakfast and hot coffee and discussed how they were going to spend the day waiting for the weather to clear.

After spending some time resting and relaxing in their hotel rooms, Sanford ventured down to the hotel's front desk to snack on some fresh apples. He struck up a conversation with the front desk clerk, saying he hoped the weather would be clear the next morning so they could depart. The clerk asked if they liked to watch hockey. Sanford said sure, and was offered two free tickets to that night's local hockey game along with the hotel shuttle to drive them to and from the arena. When Sanford returned to his hotel room, he got hold of Marv and suggested they go to a hockey game that evening. Marv, a bit confused as to how Sanford arranged that, said sure! As it turned out, it was a season game between two Canadian NHL teams. Marv and Sanford found some good seats at the arena, and realized they did not know which two teams were playing. Sanford wisely suggested they wait until the crowd around them cheers for one team or the other, just to make sure they were rooting for the right team!

With the brakes fixed on both airplanes, gear sorted, and fully fueled, they departed Kamloops as a flight of two the next morning. Or, as Canadian flight regulations say, 'the flight plus one'. They continued on through Prince George, Fort Nelson, Watson Lake, Whitehorse, Northway, Tok, and Anchorage.

Marv recalls they did encounter snow north of Cache Creek all the way to Lac La Hache, where it soon cleared. From there, they left the highway and flew the Fraser River at Williams Lake, which paralleled the highway. Their next fuel stop was at Prince George, where they departed the highway again on their way across the Peace River, with Dawson Creek and Fort St. John off to the

east. Working their way through the northern Rocky Mountain chain up to Williston Lake, they picked up the highway again between Pink Mountain and Sikanni Chief Village along the river, with their final stop for the day at Fort Nelson.

Departing Fort Nelson the next morning, they had beautiful and sunny weather with smooth flying all day. They headed west-northwest to follow the Alaskan highway and flew over Toad River Lodge that had a beautiful, well-maintained airstrip. This was an overnight stop for Marv on his driving trips, and he recalls how accommodating and friendly the owners were. They continued to climb in altitude to navigate through the pass near Stone Mountain. During World War II, there was a military camp near Stone Mountain where some remnants can still be seen.

A few miles down the road they flew across Muncho Lake, which was frozen over with ice and a nice cover of snow. That's when Sanford spotted a guy on a tractor on the lake, blowing snow off to clear a landing strip on the ice. Marv noticed that Sanford was working his way over the lake, and hailed Sanford on the radio. Marv said to leave him alone because he had his back to the airplanes and Sanford would scare him if he flew too close. Swinging off to the side, with his tires brushing the snow, Sanford flew alongside the guy on the tractor, and got a friendly smile and wave in return.

After Muncho Lake, the terrain continues to drop down toward the Liard River, which they followed all the way into a village called Lower Post, on the east-west border of British Columbia and the Yukon Territory. They followed the Liard River into Watson Lake for fuel, and continued on to the Swift River and Teslin Lake with the Johnson Crossing bridge on the north end of the lake.

Marv recalls this area on one of his driving trips years ago, seeing a Cessna airplane over Swan Lake. Further down the highway, Marv pulled off at Log Jam Creek and made some soup for lunch in his camper. After a short break, he continued driving on the highway, heading west and going uphill toward the crest of a hill. As he approached the crest, he came face to face with an airplane taking off on the highway, heading east and uphill as well, on the other side of the crest. Marv describes it as first seeing the wings materialize, then the prop, then the entire airplane as it seemed to levitate just above the road. It had just gotten airborne, and they were going to have a close encounter of the Alaska kind. Marv recalls his driver window was open a few inches and he heard the exhaust of the airplane. Then he saw the left main tire fly past his head, just outside the window!

As they approached Whitehorse, Marv remembers that the air temperature would drop down sometimes as much as 20° as he descended to just over the frozen lakes. Their final stop for the day was in Whitehorse, where they were able to stay at the historic Gold Rush Hotel. After getting settled in the hotel, Sanford and Marv noticed some other hotel patrons in the lobby, well-dressed for being outside in the sub-zero temperatures. Marv describes them as looking like the Michelin Man with bulky clothing looking much too big for their body. Inquiring with the waitress at the hotel restaurant, they discovered many Japanese tourists visit this area to be able to witness the Northern Lights, which are most spectacular at night in the heart of the winter.

According to several publications, the Yukon reportedly hosts about 4,000 to 5,000 Japanese tourists during the winter months. At all-season resorts in Alaska, owners have also reported that up to 90% of their wintertime clientele is Japanese. The reason, according to a longstanding northern rumor, is that Japanese couples flock to northern Canada to try and conceive a child under the Northern Lights. The story goes that this will give their children extra wisdom. Another version says the Northern Lights can also help an infertile couple to conceive.

Day four brought beautiful weather again for the final trek to Anchorage. Soon after departing Whitehorse, and having gained confidence in the new airplanes and engines, they decided to go cross-country rather than follow the highway. They were never very far from the highway, but far enough to be in the wilderness and mountains and frozen lakes and rivers that offered pristine beauty like none other. Their flight crossed the Donjek River and White River, both flowing eventually into the Yukon River.

With a scheduled stop to clear customs back into the U.S. at Northway, Alaska, Marv had finally made the journey he had always dreamed of. Their next stop was Tok, Alaska, for fuel. The town is commonly referred to as Tok Junction since this is where the highway now offers two options: Stay on the Alaskan Highway #1, eventually arriving in Fairbanks, or turn onto the Tok Cutoff Alaskan Highway #2, to finally arrive in Anchorage, landing at Lake Hood strip alongside the international airport.

In my personal opinion, this is the most beautiful stretch of flying of the entire trip. The flight from Tok to Anchorage usually takes about 3-1/2 hours, and it is always over way too soon. There are several mountain passes to navigate through in this stretch, including the beautiful Tahneta Pass and Sheep Mountain Pass. As we fly by Sheep Mountain, we can look over our left shoulder to see the moraine and terminus of the Matanuska Glacier as it melts into the Matanuska River. The final part of the flight follows the Matanuska River where it empties into the Knik Arm, and finally flowing past Anchorage into the Gulf of Alaska.

Marv fulfilled his dream of flying a small airplane to Alaska, and Sanford was there to see it and help make it happen. Many dream to do it, just a few actually do.

Chapter 11

The Inside Passage to the Last Frontier

From Sanford's collection:

I was lucky enough to spend a great deal of my flying career in what we call bush country. The wilderness in the northern region of the United States and Canada is beautiful but non-forgiving. Classroom training is useful, but there is no better reward in life than the real experience of successfully flying over the wilderness to destinations most people will never see or go. There are no airport terminals, airline schedules, or rental car services at the most pristine places in the world. 9-1-1 simply doesn't exist! Special planning becomes routine, life-saving survival gear becomes standard equipment. Diverting to a local airport while in route to avoid some rough weather, or stop to stretch your legs and have a soda pop, is not an option. It is definitely not for everyone. But if you are willing to step outside, where there are no warning labels that tell you how to wash your hands, in this little so-called safe world, where someone else is taking you by the hand, and leading you through life, the rewards are endless!

That being said, I would like you to ride along with me on this trip.

My next job would be very challenging, to say the least. A gentleman in Juneau, Alaska, owned a beautiful Carbon Cub on wheels, and needed it flown to Washington State to install a brand-new set of floats. He was the first one to purchase this style of amphibious floats for this model of airplane, with wheels that could be extended out of the bottom of the floats, making both runway landings at airports and water landings possible. The floats were now ready, and the excitement and urgency to transport his airplane to Washington, had now arrived. I packed my survival gear, along with my toothbrush, and caught the next available jet to Juneau.

This is a very unique part of the United States, to say the least. It is the capital city of the great State of Alaska, and is not directly accessible by roads. The Pacific Ocean is to the west, and the majestic Boundary Ranges of the Coast Mountains lies to the east, dividing and providing a natural border between the United States and Canada. It is a pristine landscape that is home to more wildlife than any place else in the world.

I departed within an hour of arriving in Juneau, and within the next 15 minutes, I was flying over two humpback whales that were playing and feeding in the ocean. The size of these beautiful animals is unbelievable. The rest of my trip was amazing, and I was blessed with perfect weather for my flight south. It is rare to have a clear day in the Inside Passage, since it is surrounded by ocean waters and mountain ranges, constantly causing two very distinct and different climates to collide.

I landed for the night at Port Hardy, British Columbia. The next morning, I flew to Friday Harbor, Washington, and cleared customs back into the U.S. Just two more short hours, and this beautiful trip was over. I wanted to do it again soon! I felt lucky to have blue skies and calm winds while flying the Inside Passage through Alaska and British Columbia, and it provided another huge deposit in my bank of memories.

After the floats were installed on the Carbon Cub, I did some flight testing to be sure they were ready to go. Anxious to have another adventure of a lifetime, I was off again heading back to Juneau. I cleared Canadian customs, and flew north over the ocean. But this time I had a false sense of security underneath me with the newly-installed floats. If something went wrong, I could land on the ocean. But then what? It would just prolong the inevitable, with no cell phone service, no help, no sand beaches, just jagged rocks with waves crashing onto the shore. No worries!

I landed again at Port Hardy, British Columbia, for the night. The next morning, another beautiful day greeted me with blue skies and calm winds. The sights were spectacular! I saw many ships of all sizes, from small fishing boats to huge passenger cruise ships, traveling to and from Juneau. After an hour of some of the nicest weather I have ever seen, I realized all good things must come to an end. I could see a wall of weather just ahead. With no place to land, and trying to stay out of the clouds, I descended to only 100 feet above the water. It started to rain and the fog got worse. I had to descend further down to 20 feet over the water, with only 1/8 of a mile of visibility. My navigation equipment would keep me in the middle of the channel and away from rocks, lighthouses, and land, but now I am in the middle of the shipping lane. I slowed the airplane to a safe 50 mph to give me time to avoid flying into a ship. Straining to see through the rain on the windshield, I was trying to see anything that looked like a ship materializing through the fog.

All of a sudden, without warning, literally right beside me, a huge humpback whale breached out of the water, nearly hitting me! Think about it. If I hit a whale with the airplane, no one would ever know what happened. I would be on the bottom of the ocean, and just another missing pilot, never to be found. I continued flying on, but just a couple feet higher.

The weather finally started to improve, giving me about a mile of visibility. Since the weather was still less than desirable, I radioed ahead to the control tower at Ketchikan, Alaska, to request a special VFR (Visual Flight Rules) clearance to land.
I was able to make my appointment time to clear U.S. customs, had the airplane refueled, checked the weather, and departed with better weather ahead of me. It continued to rain, but the visibility improved and remained good.

Then I started to see something floating in the water. I deviated over to see it was a small chunk of ice. I thought to myself, what the heck is that doing out here? It wasn't long when I started to see more and more ice. As I followed what looked like a huge breadcrumb trail, I finally found the source. It was a glacier terminus that was calving huge chunks of ice out into the ocean. The warm rain was melting the ice that had been frozen for millions of years. As I flew up to the edge of the glacier, I could see sea lions on the ice chunks all along the flow, enjoying the free ride.

Again, I had no one to share this experience with, until now! Thanks for coming along!

Chapter 12

Dreaming to Fly – Flying the Dream

Ever dreamed of flying your own airplane to Alaska? Talked about it, did a flight plan, talked about it some more. Then 20 years go by and you still haven't made it happen? Same here, until a few years ago.

Sanford and I moved to the Pacific Northwest in 2007 and lived on the east side of the Cascade Mountains. We call it the dry side, and we refer to the west side (Seattle) as the 'wet' side. The weather on the east side is a pilot's dream – over 300 days of sunshine and an average of 8 inches of precipitation a year, including snow. And even when it's not sunny, the weather is usually very nice with moderate temperatures year-round and with four distinct seasons. We even had enough snow one winter morning to quickly put the skis on our Cessna and enjoy about two hours of ski flying. It wasn't long before the snow was melting and the asphalt on the runway was showing through. Sorry, I got sidetracked…that's another story.

We moved to the Pacific Northwest and found ourselves that much closer to the preferred general aviation routes to Alaska. But it still took us a few years to make the trek. Sanford's flying went from many years of pleasure to now be a career. He worked his way into test-flying Cubs and ferrying some of them from the Lower 48 (referred to as 'outside' by Alaskans) to Anchorage, Fairbanks, and Juneau. As they say, who doesn't want to grow up and be a test pilot?

Off he goes, making several one-way flights from Washington State to Anchorage, Alaska. Some in the winter with a back seat and baggage compartment filled with survival gear. These flights are not for the inexperienced and weak of heart! Sanford has many years of bush flying experience as well as flying in extreme sub-zero temperatures. Add to that mountains and weather. Plus, the weather reporting stations are hours apart with several mountain ranges to pass through harboring unknown weather conditions. No passengers on these flights, and no cell phone service. It didn't take me long to figure out we should have a satellite tracker, just in case…but again, another story!

As luck would have it, spring happens every year. And this year when it did, I was in luck! There was now room in the back seat for a passenger, and I got dibs! Imagine sitting in the back seat of a Cub with big-screen-tv windows on each side. Three solid days of flying with the beauty of nature at its best, just beyond the wing tips. Ever-changing scenery and wonderful companionship, there was never a moment of boredom.

Fast forward to this year's trip that turned into a round trip in two airplanes – one Cub going up, and another coming back. Weather conditions were amazing. We caught blue skies and a bit of a tail wind, and decided we were in the running to fly the Trench. Being one of the favored general aviation routes, it is located within the Rocky Mountain Trench in Central British Columbia, Canada, with the southern point at Mackenzie, British Columbia (CYZY) and the northern point at Watson Lake, Yukon Territory (CYQH). A major part of the Rocky Mountain Trench is Williston Lake. Amazingly this is a man-made lake that was formed when the W.A.C. Bennett Dam was built in 1968. It is over 350 nautical miles between Mackenzie and Watson Lake, with Williston Lake alone being about 124 nautical miles long.

On the north end of Williston Lake are some smaller fresh-water lakes that offer a stunning appearance. The lakes have crystal clear cobalt-blue water and many hold small islands within their shores. Surrounding each island, submerged just under the surface, is an emerald green glow that is an unbelievable sight. The glow, we find out, is caused by finely-crushed granite (sand) that creates what I like to believe is a glowing halo. Our Guardian Angels are saying hello.

There are a few remote air strips along the Trench that lend some comfort should an unscheduled stop be necessary. But they are truly remote with no services and no fuel, so they are not your first choice should you have any issues, mechanical or otherwise. Fuel management became top priority, gauging the best winds aloft and keeping a straight line. In the meantime, I was not prepared to see such beauty and gorgeous scenery and wildlife. The concern of fuel and winds quickly slipped away to my amazement of our surroundings. And it was over way too soon. At just over four hours, it was one of the longest legs I have flown in a single-engine with my husband, and it was there and gone.

But we are on a delivery and must press north by northwest. I'm pretty sure it was in that direction anyway, with the massive compass deviation that occurs that far north. I had always seen the notations on the aviation maps, but it was really something to watch.

The rest of the trip was as beautiful and spectacular as you could expect, after seeing the stunning Trench. Moose, bison, mountain goats, eagles, hawks, deer, bears, antelope, beavers, ducks, geese…wow. Too many to count and take pictures of, but I tried.

We arrived in Anchorage and landed at Lake Hood strip – what an experience! This is general aviation at its finest. They have both a land-based runway and a lake runway, both sitting within a stone's throw of the commercial Anchorage airport. The lake is unique that it is restricted to airplanes only – no boats except those designated for maintenance to keep the lake clear of weeds and debris. The general aviation arrival and departure procedures are precise and expect the pilots to be well versed. I was in good hands. And then to see the airplanes, and more airplanes, and floatplanes too many to count. General aviation is alive and well!

After a few days of relaxation and spending precious time with some great friends, we picked up our ride for the return trip from Anchorage to Washington State. A new Carbon Cub with bush tires and extended fuel tanks. This was definitely a cross-country machine. The plan was to fly the Trench again on the way home. As it turned out, we did not. I was informed by my pilot in command that we had the rare opportunity to have three days of good weather along the coast, so we decided to take this route back to the Lower 48. This was a chance of a lifetime, and it did not disappoint!

We flew south out of Anchorage to the coast, and followed it for the next two days. While it was easy for me to describe the flight through the Trench, this is beyond description. At least a description that does justice to the pristine beauty of Alaska and Canada. Where do I start.

Another long four-hour leg, again with fuel management and winds aloft being top priority. Beautiful weather, favorable winds, and again wonderful companionship, make this a trip of a lifetime. We settled in knowing we were in good shape to make the leg with no problem fuel-wise. It happened again. The concerns faded away and opened up to an experience that is beyond description. Glaciers hugged the peaks of the mountains, flowing one on top of the other with snow so perfect it looked like smooth cirrus clouds  from a distance. The glaciers made their way down the mountainside, forming their own personal lake below filled with icebergs, big and small. Some were as large as a house, on the surface. Who knows how big they were under the water. Again, cobalt-blue water as clear as imaginable. Mountain after mountain, glacier after glacier, lake after lake. And that was just to our left.

To our right, the ocean. Flat calm and sparkling in the sun. A nice sandy beach to separate the land from the sea, lending a place for the eagles to sit and watch for their next catch in the water. In some places two eagles would perch together, undaunted and uninterested in the airplane. We watched sea lions and whales. To look ahead was miles and miles of the same. Then it dawned on me – no people, no houses, no roads. No indication whatsoever of civilization. It was just us with the untouched beauty that only Mother Nature can offer. We had it all with mountains on one side and the ocean filled with creatures on the other. We really had it all. But wait, was that a waterfall I just saw?

Yes, it was, and we decided to go investigate. With camera in hand, we flew up one of the largest glaciers we have ever seen. It had surrounded its own lake, with a large island in the middle. A long deep bay paralleled the coastline and was where I had seen the waterfall. As we flew in closer, we discovered another waterfall, and another. We realized the entire bay was surrounded with nothing

but waterfalls coming from the glacier itself. One waterfall dropped several hundred feet, pounding its way underground and back out just below. Another seemed to split apart half way down only to merge again before hitting the lake.

Then a curious sight… it looked like a sheet of gray-colored water coming over the edge. This waterfall had to be a couple hundred feet wide and was a massive sheet of water falling a thousand feet down into the lake.

We continued flying out of the bay toward the main lake, hoping to see the glacier calving and catch it on video. Then back over glacier ice with crevasses deep and wide enough to swallow a car completely out of sight. Miles and miles of ice.

A couple of days later, and after many more spectacular sights, we arrived back in the Lower 48. We are flying high on life and feeling so fortunate that everything came together so that we were able to accomplish this trip. Back to reality, and clearing U.S. Customs was in order. After being told that we could not clear at our first-choice airport Friday Harbor (KFRH) in Washington State, we were redirected to Bellingham airport (KBLI). We have flown internationally for nearly 30 years, before and after 9-11. In all our years and encounters with U.S. Customs, we have never been so shocked and humiliated as we were upon arriving in Bellingham, Washington.

After being courteously greeted by a Customs officer at the airplane, we proceeded into the office with his permission to call FAA Flight Service and cancel our flight plan. As we walked into the office, and as Sanford was just getting connected with Flight Service, the second officer greeted us by pointing and shouting at us, demanding we hang up the phone. We were then told to go outside to make the call, so we turned around to leave. We were yelled at again to return and not leave without permission. What? With Sanford's face expressing the full disgust of the situation, he hung up the phone (and yes, hung up on the FAA) and questioned the rude and unacceptable treatment we were receiving. The result? More shouting saying: "Do I have to handcuff you? Just stand there and be quiet!" Wow, all that in about 20 seconds.

Upon the completed review of our credentials (finally), our passports were literally thrown back at us across the counter and landed on the floor. We were rudely given permission to leave the office and return to the airplane. How's that for a welcome home for two law-abiding

U.S. citizens? And yes, for those pilots who have flown internationally as well, we did file e-APIS the night before.

All that behind us, we were determined it would not ruin our entire trip. How could it? We had just seen what so few humans get to see, from an airplane, sharing the incredible time with each other. It just doesn't get any better.

On Monday, I returned to my day job, and friends at the office graciously asked: "How was your vacation?"

Where do I start?

Chapter 13

Taking the Southern Route

From Sanford's collection:

A call came in, and an aircraft in southern Florida needed to be delivered to California before Christmas, and Santa Claus was busy with other things. As Diane was snowplowing in Washington State, I was on a commercial flight to sunny Florida expecting a nice trip from the East Coast to the West Coast in nice warm weather. The next morning, I arrived at the airport to pick up the airplane and planned to depart at first light. Not so sunny as it turned out, with a 300-foot ceiling of broken clouds. Not that bad to take off in, but at a busy airport, they need better weather. After 30 minutes, the tower granted me special permission to take off.

I quickly found a hole to climb up through and departed Florida in the sunshine. This beautiful airplane had small fuel tanks that limited my flight legs to three hours, which meant I would be making many fuel stops. Traveling north to the top of Florida, I had calm winds and beautiful weather. As I took a left and started heading west for

Louisiana, I began to encounter headwinds. By the time I got to Texas, I was battling a direct headwind that was blowing between 40 and 50 mph. This airplane is designed so it will fly as slow as 30 mph. If you think about it, I could have flown backwards 10 to 20 mph in these winds!

I called ahead to the airport at Hereford, Texas, and asked for help holding the airplane down while I fueled so it wouldn't take flight in the high winds. The young man said he would keep an eye out for me when I arrived. After fueling, I asked if I could depart straight out from the ramp, directly into the wind, so it would not get under a wing as I turned and flip me over. He said it would be okay since no one else was flying. I did a vertical takeoff, using only just a few feet to get airborne.

I finally had enough of this crazy wind and decided to spend the night in Moriarty, New Mexico. It was a small airport with a huge glider operation. Since they had a hangar available, I decided to take it rather than risk tying the airplane down outside on the ramp in the high winds. The airport manager was leaving for the day and gave me a courtesy car to get to the hotel. He said I could follow him, and he would show me the way into town. He pointed to a hotel right along an old highway. I went in and got a room, and found out I was on the famous Route 66. The movie industry had done some filming at this hotel many years ago. They were great people, and told me where I could find some authentic southwestern food. The next morning, I woke up to another windy day, and continued west.

I finally arrived at Bullhead City, Arizona, where the winds were calm. What a relief! After a quick refuel, I was again westbound, but the calm did not last long. Within 20 miles, I was back into the headwinds again, stronger than ever this time, and I struggled with severe turbulence. About 40 miles west of Bullhead City, there is a small mountain range about 1,500 feet high. I turned to the northwest to stay away from the highest peak. Mountain winds can be very dangerous as I have experienced in my many trips to Alaska.

I climbed to a safe altitude for crossing and put the mountain ridge safely behind me and to the southeast. Suddenly, I encountered a wind gust like I have never known in my entire career. The gust blew the airplane back toward the mountain ridge, much like putting a feather in the palm of your hand and blowing it away. I was completely at its mercy. I would guess the wind gust was somewhere between 150 and 200 mph. It hit me so hard that I actually rolled upside down, heading eastbound over 100 mph across the ground. I had no forward airspeed, so none of my controls were working. I went to full throttle to get some kind of control of the airplane, but the wind had a firm hold of me. It was blowing me backwards, straight for that 1,500-foot ridge, and there wasn't a thing I could do about it.

Somehow, I got a little control and managed to get the nose down slightly. Trying to regain control while speeding toward the ridge, I pulled from all of my acrobatic skills I had in my tool box. I was now at a 90° angle with a little nose down attitude and at full throttle. If I hit the mountain, by the time I got to the bottom of that 1,500-foot ridge, I would have been crumpled up like a little yellow tinfoil ball. I braced for impact, and at the same time, I asked for help. As I pulled the stick all the way back, I looked up and out the right window, and I watched my right tire miss the rocks by less than a foot. I flew straight down the side of the ridge to gain airspeed, and I was able to regain full control. I had to look backwards out the right window to see if my tail was still on, and it somehow was! I continued flying east while climbing to an altitude of 2,000 feet above that mountain ridge. As I crossed over the top again, I had a good look at what could have been my final resting place. It took about 15 minutes to shake that one off, and yes, I did give thanks!

Continuing west, I planned on spending the night at Bakersfield, California. My last chance to get fuel before Bakersfield was an airport called Barstow-Daggett, that is out in the middle of nowhere. I have been there before, and I learned a little about the history at that airport. During the Cold War, our government sold aircraft to the Russian government, and they would bring the airplanes to Barstow-Daggett since it was so isolated. They would have the airplanes re-stenciled in Russian language. It was a top-secret operation. When finished, the airplanes were flown up through the Alaskan route, landing at Canadian airports along the way that we – the United States – paid to have built. The airplanes were then flown across Alaska, across the narrow Bering Strait, and delivered to Russia. We were pretty sneaky back then!

Again, I called ahead and had two people from the airport come outside to hold the airplane so I could fuel it in the high winds. Once fueled, I got in and they pushed me straight back on the ramp. I thanked them and started the engine. Standing on each side of me, they both got their phones out to video my vertical takeoff, and it was! Next stop, Bakersfield, but first I had to navigate around all of the restricted airspace, such as Edwards Air Force Base. As I rounded the last restricted area and turned to the north, I had just one last obstacle to get past. It was a storm over the mountain range 30 minutes south of Bakersfield. I have an iPad I use with very modern navigation and weather technology apps. The radar showed I had to go west to get around the mountain and weather, but it proved not to be true. The weather did not give me a break. With no airports nearby, and only 1-1/2 hours of daylight remaining, it looked like I was going to have to find a country road to land and spend the night in the airplane. As I was searching for a place to land, I saw the freeway that turned out to be Interstate 5. Looking at my charts, I noticed the freeway went right through a mountain pass. This might be my ticket home, so I headed directly to the pass. Following the interstate to take a look, I discovered I could easily get through. The pass was very narrow with steep mountains on each side, but the visibility was good.

After I got through the pass, I proceeded to follow the highway downhill towards the valley. But the closer I got to the valley on the north side of the mountain, the worse the weather got and the harder it rained. Quickly, I was only 200 feet above the very busy interstate road, and it was too narrow to make a turn. Suddenly, I flew right into clouds and lost visible ground contact. I quickly pushed the stick forward to regain visibility and found the road again. But I was so low I was dangerously close to the cars and trucks. Then I lost all contact with the ground again. The only thing I could do was to go to full throttle and climb straight up, keeping my position on the GPS centered over the interstate on the map. I climbed until I got to 8,500 feet and leveled off. It was time to let the autopilot fly the airplane and give me time to breathe. A second time today, I asked for help!

The autopilot is a pilot's friend and will fly the airplane without hesitation, because it has no fear. Now safely above the mountain terrain, I looked out the window to see that I was quickly picking up ice on the airplane and was not out of trouble yet. I saw on my GPS, I was now north of the mountain and over the valley with lower terrain, so I let the autopilot fly me down to 5,000 feet. Still in the clouds but out of the ice, I needed to get safely down where I can see something again. I changed the frequency on the radio and was ready to call the airport approach controller.

Just then, I looked out my right window, and saw a tiny hole through the clouds that went all the way to the ground. I chopped the power, turned off the autopilot, and went down through the tiny hole. Fifteen minutes later, I landed at Bakersfield, and taxied to parking where a gentleman parked me. He put the wheel chocks underneath my tires and asked me if he could be of some help. I told him I needed to park the airplane for the night, fuel the airplane, and find a hotel for the evening. He told me yes, we can do all that, and he then said: "Sir, are you okay?" I must have had that look on my face! I said yes, that I just needed a minute. He said he would go get the fuel truck and be right back. For the second time today, I gave thanks. When he returned with the fuel truck several minutes later, he parked in front of the airplane, and then I noticed I had not yet taken my seatbelt off. I can shake off one experience like that, but two in one day was just a little too much.

Once I fueled and secured the aircraft, it was time to go to the hotel. The airport office called and made a reservation for me, and arranged transportation from the airport to the hotel. All I had to do now was wait for the driver to pick me up, and my day was finally over. Yes, here comes the driver. Oh no, wait! He did not see me in the dark and took off and left. There I was, standing in the parking lot in the dark because the office was now closed, not knowing which hotel they made the reservation at, and no one around. Looks like I'll be spending the night with the airplane after all. I later found out the driver's phone battery was dead and could not call back to the hotel, so he drove around and found a guy that him let use his phone. He got better directions, came back to the airport, and had no trouble finding me because I had my flashlight out this time!

Needless to say, the next day was a lot better!

Chapter 14

THE ENGINE JUST DID WHAT?

Just when you think it's going to be a normal day, an easy day, a fun flight from Idaho to California with a new, young, eager pilot in the front seat, learning along the way…surprise!

Sanford was hired by a family of pilots in Southern California to ferry their recent purchase from Northern Idaho. Mom and dad, and both sons, are all pilots. Now the family had a decision – who was going to fly with Sanford. After much discussion, it was decided the youngest son, with the least amount of experience, would make the flight. He was eager to fly with Sanford to gain experience with a seasoned bush pilot. Plus, they were bringing home a nearly brand-new Carbon Cub that was going to be his to fly.

After doing a full walk-around and pre-flight check of the just-purchased airplane, Sanford and the young pilot took off early on a Monday morning in September – Labor Day. The day offered warm, clear skies and no wind all the way to their destination. Sanford was in the back seat and the young pilot was in the front. Lessons had already started.

They made their first fuel stop in Central Oregon after about a four-hour leg. Sanford had noticed higher-than-normal engine temperatures during the flight. On the ground, he did some checking and found tape across the oil cooler that restricted air flow in order to keep the engine oil warmer in cold temperatures. So, a-hah! The problem found and fixed.

They took off and climbed to a higher altitude because of the upcoming terrain in Southern Oregon, with very high mountains and rugged landscape. Plus, Sanford still had the engine temperature issue in the back of his mind, so altitude was a good friend. Sanford says airplanes will talk to you. You just have to listen and figure out what they are saying. He had also noticed a 'ticking' sound that was unique to this airplane. Those things combined, and Sanford was on high alert.

As most of you know, Sanford carries a Spot satellite tracker whenever he flies. Even in our own airplane because you just never know. The tracker is set up with buttons that will send text and emails with customized messages. His favorite, and the one used the most, says: "I'm okay – life is good!" Not only is it fun and interesting to follow Sanford on his trips, but it is also a precise way to know exactly where he is, just in case.

They were flying at an altitude of about 8,000 feet, but only about 3,000 feet above the terrain. They had just passed over a stretch of high, rugged mountains, and were coming up on a high plateau ahead. That's when things changed. The 'ticking' sound was no longer an issue. It was the loud 'BANG' that got Sanford's attention. Then it was the continued bang-bang-bang of the engine trying to tear itself apart and break away from the airplane.

Catastrophic engine failure.

Training and instinct set in. Sanford told the young pilot in the front seat: "It's my airplane." He was now pilot in command. From the back seat. The only flight controls he had were the stick, rudders, and throttle, which was just eliminated with the engine failure. No gauges, no airspeed indicator, no view out the windshield. Sanford immediately looked in all quadrants for a landing site and the closest civilization. They were 55 nautical miles from the nearest town, and no sign of homes in any direction. Sanford instructed the pilot to shut off the engine by pulling the mixture back (shutting the fuel off to the engine) and turning off the key. At least the engine would stop running and stop trying to tear itself from the front of the airplane. They were now a glider.

Sanford instructed the young pilot to switch the radio to the closest flight service frequency. Sanford calmly called and identified the airplane, stated his general location, and declared an emergency. They had just enough altitude to hear flight service respond, and was then cut off because they were too low. So now back to landing the airplane.

Sanford spotted a gravel road on the high plateau ahead with the surrounding landscape of sagebrush and large rocks. This was his landing site. He had a slight headwind, so he started a descent that would have him touch down at the straightest part of the road. Then the wind quit, so now they glided further than he had hoped. Their new touchdown point was now a turn in the road. But that's okay, Sanford has practiced and accomplished one-wheel and one-float landings before in tight circumstances. They call it 'wearing the airplane'. He gauged the turn, their speed, their altitude, and set up for landing. But then another complication.

The young pilot in the front seat thinks differently than us in the older generation. Modern technology and social media. And an iPhone. The young pilot got his phone out and started taking video of their landing, holding the phone in both hands in the windshield. Now what little view Sanford had looking forward was completely gone! By the time he was able to have the young pilot lower his arms and move to the side, they had already touched down in the corner going about 45 mph. Blindly. Sanford was going on sight memory of the road and could only hope he gauged it right. When his view cleared, they were exactly in the middle of the road, safely on the ground. Perfect landing! Not a scratch! But they were a long way from civilization.

After they got out of the airplane, a high-five, and a smiling selfie, now they needed to figure out how to get help. The young pilot asked Sanford: "Now what do we do?" Sanford looked on the horizon and could see a cloud of dust, and said: "Look, do you see that?" The young pilot asked what that was, and Sanford said it was a vehicle. And knowing this was the only road in sight, they left the airplane on the road so they had to stop and help. Within 15 minutes they had three vehicles at the airplane. On that Labor Day, there had been a rodeo in a town on the Oregon/California border, and the ranchers and cowboys were driving the one and only gravel road in the area, on their way home.

About this time, I received an email Sanford sent from the Spot satellite tracker that said the normal, usual message: "I'm okay – life is good!" Then a second email popped in with a message that took my breath away. It was another customized message we have set up on the Spot tracker that says: "I'm okay, but I need help. Please send help." This means the airplane has mechanical issues and is on the ground, not at an airport, and he needs help. I quickly checked the tracking map and could see where they had landed. At least they were on a road, but how do I get there? I know I must be able to get there in our pickup, and my mind is racing on what gear and tools and supplies I need to take. I'm going on a road trip to somewhere in Oregon. Then a voicemail pops into my phone. It was scratchy and broken, but I could hear Sanford's voice saying they were okay and he would call me later.

One of the ranchers offered to pick up our two pilots and took them to his ranch just down the road, about 20 miles away. Seems the only spot in the house to get just one bar of cell phone service was at the end of the couch where the cat slept. The ranch itself was so isolated that when the children had sports practice for school, the drive was 80 miles each way, on gravel. And the grocery store was another 25 miles beyond the school. It gives you an idea of how isolated they were and what great timing it was for the vehicles to encounter the airplane. Like I said, timing is everything.

But the airplane was still out in the middle of nowhere, and was now the responsibility of the insurance company. They had planned to have a recovery crew retrieve the airplane the next day by taking the wings off and transporting it out on a trailer. But until the recovery crew could get there, the airplane needed to be monitored during the night to avoid vandalism. One of the ranch hands was more than happy to drive up to the airplane with cash and a case of beer to stay with it all night until the recovery crew arrived.

Here again, logistics. The closest major town was Boise, Idaho, about a five-hour drive. Not a taxi or Uber option. So, it was time to go fly again. Sanford found a crop duster from another town that was comfortable landing on the road at the rancher's house, and hired him to fly them out. Sanford was happy to see the crop duster had another airplane so they didn't have to ride in the hopper of the spray plane. They loaded up and started to taxi to the road for takeoff, but had to navigate their way through a herd of cattle. Puts a whole new meaning on open range. But the crop duster needed to return to his home and could not fly them directly into Boise. They still needed a ride. The young pilot had a friend that recently moved to Boise for a new job, so a phone call and couple of hours later, they had a ride into Boise. Sanford had an airline ticket waiting for him the next day to come home.

The airplane was successfully picked up and transported back to Yakima to Cub Crafters where it was manufactured. Sanford took some photos of the exterior of the engine after it arrived at the factory. The rod from the piston punched a hole in both the top and bottom of the engine case. Chunks of the case were missing, and cracks in the bottom of the case revealed that it was close to completely coming apart. Now, a month later, Sanford had his first look at the components that failed. The bolt holding the piston rod to the crank shaft broke and destroyed the bearing. Sanford showed me photos of the bearing, which he had to explain, because to me it looked like flat and twisted shrapnel. Sanford said it truly sent a cold chill down his spine to see the broken and destroyed parts of that engine.

So now, a new engine is installed, some regular maintenance is being done, and the airplane will soon be ready to fly again. And yes, the California family of pilots has already asked Sanford to deliver it. Like Sanford said, he has never failed to complete a delivery, so being able to finish this job was important.

Huge kudos to the original owner of the airplane. He immediately stepped up and offered the California family two options: He would completely refund the purchase price of the airplane and re-take ownership, or he would pay for a new engine to be installed, which is what they chose to do. Like the original owner said, it was just a matter of time that the engine would fail. It just happened that he sold it a few hours before. He said the most important part is that no one was hurt or killed. The rest is just airplane parts. I have so much respect for this man, and he has restored my faith in humanity. Oh, and another thing I like about the original owner is his email signature: "You can't fix stupid, but you can numb it with a 2 x 4!" How can you not like this guy!

I just love the aviation industry and its people.

Chapter 15

Delivery Service

We have done some unique and fun things with the airplane, including deliveries of unique items for unique reasons.

Early in Sanford's flying career, when it was still considered old-school flying and navigating, many airports had fly-in events and flight breakfasts to bring in pilots and airplanes from around the area. They were great fund raisers, and many times the local fraternal clubs provided the equipment and staff to cook for the airport guests.

Quite often the airport would have contests for the pilots to participate and compete in. There were flour-bombing contests to see who could get closest to the 'X' on the field. A couple cups of flour or so was put in a brown paper bag and closed. The pilot would fly over the target as low and slow as possible, and took their best guess when to drop the flour. The bag would pop open upon impact, making a white spot on the ground along with a cloud of flour. They would also have spot-landing contests to see who could touch down, and stay on the ground, closest to a line on the runway. No adding power once they were set up for landing, so the pilot had to know their airplane and judge the wind to set up their distance, glide, and altitude just right.

Another fun and challenging contest was to have the pilot circle the airport at a specific altitude, and a helium balloon would be released from the ground. The pilot would try to pop the balloon with the propeller as quickly as possible. But remember, there are always winds at altitude so the balloon would drift as well as continue to climb. If the pilot missed, he would turn the airplane around as quickly as possible, find the balloon, and try to catch up to it again. The number of tries the pilot got depended on how proficient he was turning and climbing the airplane, not to mention just finding the balloon each time.

My favorite contest uses gravity to induce the challenge for the competition. The pilot would climb their airplane to a specific altitude, open a window, and throw out a roll of toilet paper. They needed to unroll several feet of paper before releasing it so it would unroll as it dropped, leaving a long white streamer above it. The challenge was to see how many times the pilot could cut the paper streamer before the roll of toilet paper hit the ground. Turning the airplane quickly and finding the paper streamer took quite some skill and finesse. I always had to laugh when Sanford would return and have pieces of toilet paper stuck in the tail of the airplane.

Sanford was really good at these kinds of contests. Over the years, he honed his skills with several different airplanes and different commodities as well. It did not matter what the wind was doing or in what direction. He could calculate the forward speed of the airplane and the drift of the wind and usually come out the winner. This proved to pay off in several deliveries we have made over the years. Here are just a few.

We were sitting at home one spring on a Saturday morning, and we got a call from a friend who was on an island just outside of town in Minnesota. He had gone up the lake to an island a couple weeks before while the ice was still safe. His project was to build a new dock at the cabin, and the late winter ice made a good platform to walk out on. Spring was well on its way to the area, and with the warmer weather the ice would only support a person or two, not a heavier vehicle. He was nearly done, but he ran out of bolts, washers, and nuts that he needed to finish the dock before his ice walkway disappeared.

This sounded like fun, and we were more than happy to help. We were tasked with going to the local hardware store and buying all the 5-inch and 6-inch bolts with washers and nuts we could find. With a bag full of hardware – way more than even a double-bag could support – away we went to the airport. It was still pretty cold, so we decided to leave the passenger door on the airplane.

The bay where we needed to drop the very heavy package was surrounded by the island on three sides. This made flying low enough and slow enough into the bay a challenge, as we still needed enough speed and altitude to climb up and over the terrain of the island once the drop was made. Sanford circled the island a couple of times to size it up and determine a flight path, and we were now on the final bombing run.

As we approached, Sanford instructed me to open the door and slide the package outside the airplane, but hang onto it. We had bagged the bolts and washers and nuts in several layers of sacks, with the final bag being a heavy-duty garbage bag. It was black so it would be easy to see on the bare ice surrounding the island. As we approached the drop point, we could see the ice was dark and honey-combed, which means it was thin and deteriorating. We worried the bag would actually break through the ice and sink to the bottom, but we had to try.

Sanford gave me a countdown to the drop point, and then called for me to drop the package. I could watch it out the open door for a short while, long enough to see it hit the ice and slide toward the island. Success! Sanford put the power in and we climbed up and out of the bay. He came back around and circled over the bay, and we could see our friend walking out on the ice to pick up the package. He was carrying a long pole horizontally, much like a tight rope walker, in case the ice gave way and he broke through. This would keep him afloat and able to climb out on top of the ice and get to safety. Luckily everything went well, and he was able to get the package and finish the dock. As I remember, it was only another day or two before the ice was completely gone that year, and our friend returned to the mainland by boat. Job well done!

Every winter we were invited to go to a ski plane fly-in in December or January. The exact dates always depended on how cold the temperatures had been and if there was enough ice on the lake to make it safe for the weight of the airplanes. It was always a fun time and great to see other pilots that we had made acquaintance with over the years.

Just up the hill from the lake, there was always a bonfire near the hunting shack owned by the host of the fly-in. Inside he would have the wood stove going and a pot of chili or soup. Everyone brought hot dogs or bratwurst to roast on the bonfire for lunch. Some years when it was sunny and cold, it was a great way to spend the entire day, even when the high temperature for the day was still below zero. Northern Minnesota in the winter: Brutal but beautiful.

As we headed to the fly-in one year, we realized we forgot our lunch on the kitchen counter at home. We were very close to the destination so turning around to pick it up didn't make sense, because not too far away from the fly-in was a small town and a lake right along the main highway. It was populated along the shoreline with a few cabins, two restaurants, a hotel, a gas station, a grocery store, and one recently installed stoplight. Time to make a quick stop for groceries in Orr, Minnesota, population 249.

The Orr airport was too far to land and walk into town. Since we were on skis, Sanford decided to land on the lake along the highway. There was a boat launch directly behind the grocery store, and the parking lot was well covered in snow. The boat launch also had good snow cover on it, so it made for a good ramp from the lake to the parking lot. After a beautiful landing, Sanford lined up the airplane, gave it more power, and up the boat ramp we went! He found a nice wide parking spot for the airplane, we parked, did our grocery shopping, and headed to the fly-in. While we were there, we noticed several people pointing and taking pictures of the airplane. Haven't they seen an airplane in the grocery store parking lot before?

As we were roasting our bratwurst over the bonfire, we noticed our host had an abundance of small winter birds constantly flying and hanging around the hunting shack. He likes to feed the birds with suet-like product and hangs it from a tree. The birds were so happy and enjoying the feast you could nearly walk up and touch them as they were feeding. It turns out the feeder hanging on a wire in the tree was a beaver carcass. Beaver hunting and selling pelts was, and still is, very popular in Northern Minnesota. And the carcass is not wasted and is returned to nature. But our host was having trouble finding more beaver carcasses and asked if we knew anyone that traps beaver. And we did.

Another delivery with the airplane was in order since the hunting shack could not be accessed by car or truck. We talked with our next-door neighbor, who was a beaver trapper, and he saved the next carcass for us. Wrapped and triple-bagged in black garbage bags that are easy to see on the ice and in the snow, we loaded up the airplane and away we went the next weekend.

As Sanford made his parcel-drop approach into the lake, we wanted to get the package as close to the shoreline as possible. It was heavy and bulky and hard to carry, plus the hunting shack was up a steep hill. I thought I needed a little extra time to get the door open and the package outside since it was so large and heavy. So as Sanford was coming around to fly a straight line toward the shack, I got the bag outside and waited for instructions to drop.

I was actually able to get the bag outside much quicker than I anticipated, so the length of time it was hanging out of the airplane was a little longer than normal. As we were flying toward the drop point, I noticed the bag was stretching with the weight of the carcass in the wind. I was now worried the bag would break and I would lose the package too far out on the lake! The bag stayed intact just long enough for the successful drop of the package. It hit the ice on the lake and slid right up to the shoreline. I figure the bag was about eight to ten feet long before I let it go…it had stretched that much. Whew!

Sanford had been flying skis on the airplane for several winters now, and we had figured out some tricks that helped us maneuver the airplane on the ground. When the airplane is on skis, the tail wheel is mostly ineffective in the deep snow. We used to use a tail-wheel ski, but it proved to be more of a hinderance than useful. The only steering is speed and enough wind on the tail and rudder, so a turn requires a much larger area. With the airplane on wheels and on hard surface, a turn could be done nearly within the axis of the airplane using much less power and brakes for steering.

Our solution was to tie a 20-foot-long rope to the tail wheel of the airplane. We just let it dangle in flight since it did not cause any issues with the back of the airplane. Then when we landed and needed to make a tight turn, it was available for his new power steering assistant, named Diane.

Sanford would land and stop near the area to turn. I would climb out of the airplane and walk to the back and pick up the rope. The length was nice so that I could get to either side and stay out of the prop wash. I would hate to guess what the wind chill was like in that prop wash on those cold, beautiful winter days already below zero! I would then get to either side so that Sanford had a visual of me. I gave him the thumbs up and he put the power in to raise the tail of the airplane. It was just enough to make the tail 'fly' without moving the airplane ahead much. With the tail in the air, I would pull the rope and swing the tail of the airplane around to get him pointed in the right direction. This worked good in really tight spots, especially parking near other airplanes on frozen lakes.

It never failed that someone would notice that we had a rope tied to the tail wheel. They instantly assumed we had forgotten to untie the airplane and was dragging the rope along accidentally. This had happened so often it was time to have a little fun with it. A trip to the store and we were ready for our next ski plane fly-in.

A beautiful, clear sunny day with temperatures in the mid 20's greeted us the next weekend for another ski plane fly-in. We had bought a small dog collar, pretty and pink with lots of sparkles on it. We buckled it and tied it to the end of the rope. Then when we were approached at the fly-in, we were prepared for the people who took pride in informing us we forgot to untie the airplane before taking off.

Sanford would rush to the end of the rope, pick it up, and in absolute horror say: "Oh no! Fifi! We forgot about Fifi!" I always liked to add: "I'm hungry…let's go eat. We can look for her on the way back."

We're not sure, but we think some did not realize we were joking!

During one of the long, cold winters in Northern Minnesota, we found ourselves with an open weekend and no plans. The weather was forecasted to be snowy with poor visibility, so we did not plan to fly anywhere. Saturday's weather proved to be just that and Sunday's forecast had not changed. However, when we woke up Sunday morning, we had a bright and clear day. Now we needed to figure out somewhere to fly.

We quickly remembered a friend had told us about a ski plane fly-in on a lake just over the border in Wisconsin. It was a bit further than we normally liked to travel for a day trip, so we were going to need fuel before returning home. Sanford made a phone call to the airport closest to the lake to make sure they would be open for fuel. But we had a bigger problem of how to get to the fuel pump with dry asphalt, no wheels, and flat skis designed to slide on snow. More on that in a bit.

When we arrived at the lake, we were surprised to find a beautiful resort with a new restaurant that was celebrating their grand opening. It turns out that was the reason for the fly-in. They even had a live radio show broadcasting from the resort to advertise the opening. We landed on the ice and walked up to the restaurant and were quickly greeted by the restaurant manager. They saved us the best seat in the house, near the windows looking onto the lake. Brunch was free for us since they appreciated that we flew in for the celebration. Wonderful food and hosts!

As it happened, they planned a couple of flying contests for the pilots and airplanes. A drop contest and a spot-landing contest. With Sanford's skills, we were a shoe-in to win! We needed a partner for the drop contest so we solicited a local young man that we had been chatting with about airplanes. He thought it would be great fun and readily agreed to be on our team. We were given three softball-size colorful balls made of plastic. Our teammate was to stay on the ground and was given a huge sturgeon-size fishing net. Scratching our heads and looking a bit puzzled, the game organizer explained that we drop the balls out of the airplane, one at a time on each pass, and our teammate on the ground tries to catch the balls in the net. Got it! We huddled to set up our game plan, and Sanford instructed our teammate to just stay put out on the lake and not chase the airplane. We would drop the ball close enough so that he should not have to move but a few steps to catch the ball.

First pass. I have the window open with the ball in hand ready to drop. I am given the countdown and drop the ball on cue. I then look out the window to watch and see if we are successful. I can now see our teammate running for all he is worth, chasing the airplane! He doesn't realize Sanford has adjusted for the wind and drift of the ball until it is about half way down. Then all of a sudden, he stops and starts running back the other direction toward the spot he was supposed to stay at. Last I could see, was him taking a huge leap with the fishing net extended way in front of him and his feet in the air! I couldn't tell if he caught the first ball in the net.

Second and third passes. Same as above, only this time our teammate decided to stay put. I drop the ball, he takes a few easy steps, and successfully catches the ball in the net. Well, we at least got two out of three catches. We landed and were greeted by a very excited teammate. Three for three! We won!

Now the next contest is a spot-landing contest. They painted a wide red line in the snow and the goal was to land with the axles of the skis as close to the line as possible, and keep the airplane firmly on the ground. Since we were closest to the landing site, we were called on to be the first airplane to compete. Sanford lined up the airplane, set his glide path, judged the wind, and landed the airplane on the lake. He perfectly centered the axles of the skis on the red line. Bullseye! We won again!

Getting back to my reference above about getting fuel at the nearby airport on skis. Following our success at the drop and landing contests, we decided we better head home as it was getting late in the afternoon. We needed to have good daylight to land at our base airport since it was such a small area, and the winter days were quite short that time of year.

We headed to the airport and found the area they suggested we land on skis. It was parallel to the main runway, but interrupted by a perpendicular taxiway not too far down the runway. This made our landing site quite short, but with Sanford's skills and the deeper snow we had no problem getting stopped well before the taxiway. We now have a snow ridge between us and the taxiway about two feet high where the snow had been plowed to the side. The only way to get over it and on the taxiway, and to the fuel pump, was with power. Sanford added power and got the airplane moving forward just enough, and we gently went up and over the snow ridge. What we didn't realize was the taxiway was glare ice so we slid completely across the taxiway, over the snow ridge on the other side, and back into the deep snow pointing in the wrong direction!

Time for the power steering assistant called Diane. I got out of the airplane, grabbed the rope, and moved to the side of the plane so Sanford could see me. I knew he was going to have to power up again to get back over the snow ridge and challenged to turn down the taxiway and not go back over the other side. I put a full wrap of the rope around my gloved hand and gave him the thumbs up. Power up, tail up, and I gave a good tug to set him up for a 45° entry into the taxiway. What I didn't expect was that I broke through a layer of snow and fell over as I was pulling the tail of the airplane around. Thinking I would have to get up and give it another tug, Sanford powered up more because I had turned him just enough. Problem was, the rope was still wrapped around my hand. Next thing I know I am on my feet and skating behind the airplane on the icy taxiway!

I was finally able to unwrap my hand and could see that Sanford had things well under control. He gently taxied up to the fuel pump, well within range of the fuel hose. While he has pumping fuel, I looked over at the airport office to see several people standing at the window. I'll bet they got a good laugh watching me skate behind the airplane. I know I did. I'll have to remember to sell tickets the next time!

One fall we got a call from a friend who was deer hunting with a group at a remote hunting shack. He was using a cell phone, and the service was spotty. There was no snow on the ground yet, but it was November and getting cold. The only access into the hunting shack was several miles of swamp and muck by four-wheeler. But that's what kept the land around the hunting shack so pristine. It was difficult enough to keep a lot of human traffic out of the area. And the hunting was good.

The phone call was to let us know that they had run out of beer and cigarettes, and it was still several days before they would return to civilization. They wanted the beer to celebrate the good hunting, and they had decided this was not the time to quit smoking. After finding out what brand of beer they drank and cigarettes they smoked, we made a grocery store run.

Paper grocery sacks work well for lighter objects, but this was a combination of both light and heavy. Sanford had to package things up so that both would survive the drop. Some creative packaging and layers of bags was done, with the final bag being – yep, you guessed it – the black garbage bag.

Sanford tied it with plenty of air inside to help cushion the impact. But this made it larger and harder to get out the door. Because of the wind going past the airplane, you can only physically open the door a few inches, no matter how hard you push. We had to figure out another delivery chute.

The windows on our airplane tilt open at the bottom with a bracket and hinge that only lets it go so far. But if you unhook the bracket and hinge, the window will actually open all the way up against the bottom of the wing. And it will stay there in the wind, so now we had a much bigger space to push the package out.

Sanford is all lined up for the delivery pass. Nice and slow, nice and low, but there are a lot of trees surrounding the hunting shack and not much open area. We had to be precise so as not to put the package in the trees or on the roof. I had the package ready to throw, and when Sanford says now, out it goes. It landed between the shack and the nearest pine tree, perfectly in the front of the shack. They were very happy hunters, even though they needed to let the beer sit a while before opening them. We did, however, keep them cold until delivery.

Early on when Sanford and I were still dating, it was his dad's birthday. Sanford had found a really nice sweater for his dad, and it was time to give him his birthday present. We wrapped it in a plastic bag to keep it clean, and then in some really nice and really heavy wrapping paper. But that still wasn't enough. We found a roll of crepe paper that said 'Happy Birthday' all over it, and tied streamers onto the package.

Off we go to deliver the package, which was a about a two-hour flight. And then we planned to spend the rest of the day with Sanford's folks. They lived in Southern Minnesota on a small farm, so there was plenty of yard area to make the drop. The hard part was getting his dad out of the house and into the yard so he knew his present had arrived. This was well before cell phones, plus we wanted it to be a surprise.

A few low passes by the house were in order. We had used this method before to get his folks' attention to get a message to them. This airplane also had windows that tilted out from the bottom. So once his folks were outside, Sanford would fly over, pull the throttle back to an idle in the airplane, open the window, and shout: "Pick us up at the airport!" Worked like a charm.

Sanford's mom and dad were now in the yard, expecting us to need a ride from the airport. But when Sanford made the delivery pass, he instead shouted "Happy Birthday" out his window and I threw the package out the other window. The streamers looked great and the package landed in the middle of the yard. Sanford's dad showed up at the airport wearing the sweater, which looked great on him!

Everybody likes donuts. Especially fresh donuts. And even more so when you are in a remote lake on a fishing trip for an entire week. A group of friends had left a few days earlier on their annual trip to a fly-in fishing camp, and it was time for fresh donuts.

We made a trip to the local donut shop and picked up two dozen donuts. Remember, these guys had been out there nearly a week, eating the same thing every day for breakfast, lunch, and supper. We bagged them again using the paper bags inside and the standard black garbage bag outside. It was inflated with enough air to help cushion the impact plus it had to be water-tight and float. After all, this time we were delivering donuts to a lake that was not frozen.

Sanford had done this several years in a row for our friends' annual fishing trip. And each time his accuracy was spot-on. The challenge was finding the right boat on the lake to make the donut drop. But this year the guys in the boat thought it would be funny to play hide and seek, so when they heard the airplane in the area, they took the boat to the shoreline and hid under some overhanging trees. Sanford flew over the lake a couple of times and could not find our friends. They were fairly easy to spot, because one of the guys wore a very unique hat.

Sanford checked the cabin area and could see the boats were not at the dock, so he knew they were somewhere on the lake. Now knowing they were hiding, he left the area for a short while. Apparently, our friends figured the coast was clear and came out of hiding, back out into the middle of the lake. About that time, Sanford was in stealth mode and came in over the trees and shoreline of the lake on a direct path to the boat. Out went the package, and it landed just behind the boat. All they had to do was get the dip net and pick the package out of the water.

Later in the afternoon, the fishermen returned to the cabin and put on a fresh pot of coffee. There was another group staying in the roomy cabin with them, and they were not aware of this annual tradition.

When they returned to the cabin, they were talking about an airplane that flew low over the lake and wondered if there was a problem. About that time, they noticed the pot of coffee and fresh donuts on the kitchen table. Asking how they got fresh donuts, our friend responded saying: "I have them flown in every year." Since it was obvious the other group did not believe the story, our friend said: "You saw the airplane, right? Want a donut?"

Just recently we were having dinner with some very good friends that we are lucky to have as neighbors. They were talking how their children and grandchildren were coming to celebrate Easter with them in a couple of weeks. Grandma and Grandpa always get the plastic Easter eggs and fill them with coins and candy for the grandchildren to find in the yard. After hearing a few of our delivery stories, we all decided the Easter Bunny would have to arrive by airplane this year.

Keeping the eggs from popping open on impact was a concern, so Sanford suggested each egg be wrapped in aluminum foil to keep them closed. Plus, they would sparkle in the air and be easy to find in the grass. A box of about two dozen plastic Easter eggs, wrapped in foil, were delivered to our house the day before their family arrived.

The next morning, we woke up to a clear sunny day but with high winds. It was beginning to be a concern about opening the hangar door, so the Easter Bunny arrival time had to be moved up a bit. We took off the passenger door of the airplane for this delivery, making it easier to get the box in my lap and ready for deployment.

Calculating wind direction and speed, Sanford figured out his course and drop point to adjust for the light eggs to drift in the high winds. As we approached the house, we could see the entire family outside looking up at the airplane. Fun thing was, only Grandma and Grandpa knew about the air drop. Even their adult children did not know about it.

Sanford is giving me step by step approach instructions, and we are nearly ready to drop. I get a tight grip on the box, thinking the wind would want to take it out of my hands. I didn't want the box leaving the airplane along with the eggs. As I moved the box closer to the open doorway, waiting for the instruction to drop, I could see the eggs beginning to bobble around in the box and nearly taking flight. I realized then that if I did not throw the eggs far enough out the doorway, they would blow back into the back seat of the airplane. That would be bad because we would have to come back and land, gather up the eggs bouncing around in the back of the airplane, and try it again.

So here we go, ready, ready, now! I rifled the eggs out the doorway, held onto the box, and was able to look out and watch all those sparkly eggs perfectly sprinkle throughout the yard. Sanford had made another perfect delivery. We circled and came back around to see there were five very excited grandchildren picking up Easter eggs, with their parents wondering what just happened and when did the Easter Bunny get a pilot's license.

What do you do with pumpkins the day after Halloween? Other than feed for livestock, or the possible pie or two, there must be a more creative way to use up pumpkins after Halloween. And we found it. A pumpkin-dropping contest was in order.

Our neighbor, who lived at the other end of the runway, flew a Cessna 170 just like ours. Our properties were over ten acres each so we had room to play, and we decided to set up a target and have the kids drop pumpkins. We came up with four 20-foot-long sticks of white PVC pipe and made a square target in the field. The right door came off both Cessna's and three pumpkins and an excited teenager were loaded into each airplane. The pilots made nice slow, low approaches, and the passenger decided when to drop the pumpkin. It took a few tries before they figured out the speed and drop rate of the pumpkin. And of course, it changed each time with the different sizes of the pumpkins. About the time we expected to see pumpkins splat on the ground, they would bounce! The kids got good at hitting the target, but the pumpkins would bounce 10 to 15 feet high. And with the forward motion from the airplane, they would bounce right out of the target zone. After a few tries, the kids figured out the smaller pumpkins would always bounce at least two to three times, so they started dropping the pumpkins early and let the bounces take them into the target. Nice job!

And as for the leftover pumpkins that did not get dropped, or those that survived the drop, we found another fun way to dispose of them. Ever heard of Tannerite? Yep! We hollowed out a fist-sized spot in the middle of the pumpkin, probably where you would put the nose on the jack-o'-lantern, and loaded up some Tannerite. A few practice shots on the shooting range to dial in the scope, and those pumpkins completely exploded into small chunks and the seeds came down like rain. Wonder how many wild pumpkin patches are growing there now.

Chapter 16

WEARING THE AIRPLANE

June is an amazing time of year to fly north into Canada, the Yukon Territory, and Alaska. The land of the midnight sun. Long, beautiful days with enough twilight at night that you question if you need to have the headlights on in your car. Sanford has made many trips to and from Alaska, and these two trips were with the owners along.

The first flight was in a Cessna 185 on amphibious floats from Yakima, Washington, headed to Fairbanks, Alaska. Sanford and the owner took off on a beautiful morning with the weather forecasted to be good the entire trip. With the speed and fuel capacity of this Cessna, they expected to make Mackenzie, British Columbia, Canada, the first day. They planned to arrive in Whitehorse, Yukon Territory, on day two, and then Fairbanks on day three.

By the time they arrived in Mackenzie at the end of the first day, the owner told Sanford he was experiencing some medical issues that had started soon after they departed Yakima. He was 89 years old, and he was having trouble with his blood pressure. The owner told Sanford it was quite high, and stated the exact numbers. Wondering how the owner knew exactly what his blood pressure was, Sanford found out he traveled with his blood pressure machine. That was Sanford's first clue it was going to be quite a trip.

The owner was convinced the altitude affected his blood pressure, causing it to go up, and that walking would bring it back down. Two hours at a time of walking and taking his blood pressure every 20 minutes didn't change it. Finally late on the second day, Sanford convinced him to go to the emergency room to get checked by a doctor. They gave him some medication, which was the same as he had brought along, but wouldn't take. Sanford finally got him to take it after the emergency room visit, and it brought his blood pressure down right away. After a good night's sleep, and continuing to take the medication, the owner was feeling much better. But he feared the altitude would affect it again, so Sanford had quite a time convincing him it was best to keep moving and get home to his personal doctor as soon as possible.

The rest of the flight went as expected, and the closer they got to Fairbanks, the better the owner felt. I know we have all experienced that. We stayed in touch, and the owner told us he visited his doctor soon after getting home. He just needed a couple of adjustments in his medications. Then about two weeks later, the owner let us know that he had successfully ran in a 10k race and finished! Did I mention he was 89 years old? Good for him!

A quick hop to Anchorage on a commercial flight and into another airplane to fly back to Washington State. Again, flying with the owner, this was a Piper Super Cub going to its new home. The owner was a good pilot, but did not have much time in this airplane. His good common sense told him this was too big of a trip to tackle alone for the first time, and contacted Sanford to ferry the plane from Anchorage to Spokane, Washington. As he does with most owners, Sanford offered the ride-along to the Super Cub owner as a way to get a lot of experience in this airplane in just a few days. Plus, he got to ride along with an experienced and talented bush pilot, who could show him technique and flying tips. He quickly accepted!

With the owner in the front seat and Sanford in the back, they departed on their way home. Sanford tells me the owner flew very well and by the book. Standard climb rate, standard speed, and set his altitude at the standard 3,500 feet. All good.

Then the infamous question came up. The owner asked Sanford to give him any pointers and information that could help. Sanford asked him if he was sure, and to be careful what you ask for. The owner said absolutely, so first Sanford told him to descend, but don't hit the trees. The owner laughed and said, okay, but what altitude do you really want me to fly at? Sanford said he wanted him to fly low enough that beavers would slap their tail on the water as they flew over the pond! They did, too!

The next three days were full of flying near winding rivers, through mountain passes, over clear blue lakes, and along the Alaskan highway. This type of flying helped increase the owner's skill of coordination with the controls, managing speed and altitude, and learning the airplane well enough to sense what needed to be done instead of relying on gauges. All the while managing things to watch for – beavers (of course), moose, antelope, bears, birds, and power lines. Yes, power lines.

Sanford always tells other pilots: "This is what I am going to do, but don't follow me." He does this so that inexperienced pilots don't get a bit of courage and get themselves into a situation they are not ready for.

They were flying along the river that paralleled the Alaskan highway. Sanford told the owner to get his camera out and that he would fly the airplane from the back seat. Knowing exactly where they were, and what was ahead, it was time for another lesson. Sanford was flying when the owner realized there were power lines immediately ahead. Sanford responded instantly to drop the nose of the airplane and go under the wires!

So now it was time to review. Sanford asked the owner what he would have done when he saw the power lines. His answer was to pull up and go over them, which is instinctively what most pilots would do. Sanford explained that the lines were too high and they would not have made it over. So going under them was the safest and best response. When they arrived home, Sanford described the owner's newly-gained ability and experience, saying he wore the airplane, as if they were one. Well done.

Lesson learned? Always watch for power lines when flying low. Another lesson learned? Always have Sanford in the back seat!

Chapter 17

Every Airplane has a Story

The aviation community is relatively small when compared to the population of the entire United States. Filter that even further to the general aviation community, which is considered: "Aircraft operation other than a commercial air transport or an aerial work operation." Basically, pilots flying for fun. We are always amazed when we meet new pilots and airplane owners and find out we have either met before, or we have another pilot friend in common. Pilots are consistently some of the most honest and courteous people I have ever met. They will always help someone in need. If they can't, they know someone who can. That's how Sanford has become known throughout this wonderful community.

The phone rang one day with a call from Anchorage, Alaska. A pilot had just purchased a highly-modified Piper Super Cub, a true bush plane perfect for Alaska. It was located in Pennsylvania and the new owner needed to bring it home. He did not have a lot of cross-country flying experience, and this flight from the east coast of the Lower 48, all the way to Alaska, was more than he had time for and more than he wanted to tackle alone. With the favored general aviation flying routes mainly in western Canada, this would be a coast-to-coast-to-Alaska trip. Sanford invited the owner to ride along, so he decided to have Sanford pick up the airplane in Pennsylvania and bring it to our home in Yakima, Washington. Then about a week later he planned to fly commercially to Yakima and join Sanford for the flight back to Anchorage.

Sanford flew the airplane from Pennsylvania and arrived home in Yakima three days later, having a seemingly uneventful trip. A little weather here and there, but nothing remarkable…yet. The owner flew in from Anchorage about a week later as planned, and we enjoyed a wonderful evening with him and hearing about his life and livelihood in Alaska. We only had time to hear a few of the many experiences he has had. He is in law enforcement in Anchorage, and believe me, he had some doosies!

The two of them departed the next morning with good weather and favorable winds. Sanford was optimistic they would be able to fly a beautiful general aviation route called the Trench for a three-day trip to Anchorage. Their first overnight was in Mackenzie, British Columbia, Canada, which is the south-to-north gateway through this vast terrain stretching over 400 miles. While beautiful and unique, it was also a challenge to fly the Trench since the next airport with full services was at the very northern end, more than a four-hour flight. They needed the weather to be in their favor, and it was.

The second and third days of their trip went well and without any issues. That is always a great thing when you first buy an airplane, not knowing if there are any hidden issues or concerns. The three-day trip gave the pilot a lot of time to acclimate to his new airplane and get some pointers from Sanford as well.

Usually when Sanford gets home from these trips, it takes him a few days to return to our time zone and get rested up. While on a delivery, he is always up early checking the weather, flight planning, and arrives at the airports before sunrise to pre-flight the airplanes and get a good, fresh start for the day. Many times, he will put in over ten hours of flying time a day.

The weekend arrives, Sanford is rested, and we have a chance to talk about his trip. And speaking of doosies, this one will make your jaw drop.

When Sanford arrived at our house on the first leg of the trip from Pennsylvania, the airplane needed a good cleaning inside and out. He always wants to deliver the owner's newest purchase in pristine condition, and he takes time to clean and detail the aircraft. This one needed more cleaning inside than out, which is usually not the case. After a good vacuuming and polishing, the Super Cub was ready to meet her new owner.

Well on their way the first day, the two pilots had time to talk. The owner had already shared some stories from the night before, so one more story was in order. This airplane has quite a history. One that will give you chills.

Back in the 1970's and early 1980's, a serial killer named Robert Hansen, known as the Butcher Baker killer, abducted, raped, and murdered at least 17 women in and around Anchorage, Alaska. He targeted prostitutes, would solicit and then kidnap them, and tie their hands behind their back. He would take them to the Merrill Field airport in Anchorage, load them in his airplane, and fly them to an area in the wilderness he knew well. Hansen would then release them, and then hunt them down like animals with a rifle and a knife.

Investigators suspect there were many more women, up to 30, that he killed and buried. The 17 women they found were because he had marked their burial sites on an aviation sectional map that he had hidden behind the headboard of his bed in his house. The rest of the women he confessed to killing in order to get a life sentence rather than the death penalty. But he couldn't remember where they were all buried.

By now you have probably guessed why I bring this up. This is the airplane. Imagine Sanford sitting in the back seat, hearing this story, and realizing he is sitting in the same seat as those poor victims of this serial murderer.

Since then, the airplane has been repainted and assigned new identification numbers. But the serial number remains the same. The new owner, in law enforcement, investigates everything. Before buying the airplane, he researched and found the full history of this Super Cub. In my mind, the airplane has come full circle. It is back in Anchorage where it was originally an unwilling player in many tragic deaths. And now it is in the hands of a police officer that upholds the law and captures these bad guys and sends them to jail.

Justice.

Chapter 18

SCHOOL OF HARD KNOCKS

From Sanford's collection:

They say it never rains in Southern California, but the problem is you have to get there first.

I have been introduced to a beautiful Piper Super Cub that has a desire to go to sunny Southern California, and I am just lucky enough to be the one to fly it there.

It's March and I am looking forward to seeing some sunshine. First checking the weather, and doing some flight and route planning, I see I have my work cut out for me. The numbers work out that I will be in the air for ten hours, plus time needed for stops to refuel. I will need at least three fuel stops, and may have to fly around some weather, so I need to plan extra time. At my departure point in Yakima, it will become widely-scattered lightness around 7:00 am. And the sun goes away to mostly-covered darkness at 7:03 pm at my destination in California. The fact is, I know my departure area much better than

I know my destination, so the plan is to get up and be in the air two hours before the sun comes up. Years of flying have told me to plan on the unexpected, and to always start early.

Doing my preflight the day before, and having everything ready to go early, prevents a lot of things from going wrong. On a new aircraft I have not seen before, I spend a lot of time looking it over. It is my last chance to find anything wrong before I take to the air. The first thing I look at is the paperwork. I inspect the logbook and all the legal documents that are required to be in the aircraft. Next, do a thorough walk around, looking for anything that does not look like the airplane is ready for flight. Flight controls working properly, tires inflated properly, nothing loose or hanging. These are some of the things that can really destroy my day. Next is engine inspection. Upon looking in the engine compartment and checking the oil level, I noticed a beautiful, brand-new Lycoming engine. New engines need to be cared for during the first few hours during the break-in time. They can be easily damaged if not managed properly. The tight tolerance of a new engine can cause it to run very hot and can damage the engine very rapidly. On the other hand, if it is operated with too low of a temperature, it will cause the inside of the cylinders to glaze over, and the rings do not seat properly, creating a high oil-consumption rate. Like all man-made things, this is the critical time when we find out if any of the components are defective in the engine. I like to think of it as a newborn baby that needs to be monitored at all times.

Some people need coffee to get them awake and alert, and I just happen to be one of them. But not when I am on a trip. With long-range fuel tanks on this airplane, it meant fewer stops for fuel. It also meant I could go around a lot of weather, and I liked that option. Morning coffee will have to wait.

The next morning, I was in the air when it was still as dark outside as the inside of a black-angus cow! South was the heading and climbing to an altitude where dirt did not exist, I leveled out for a speed course to California. Now I am flying over thousands of sleeping wild horses, mountains and wilderness, and there were no lights below me. Up in the distance were hundreds of red lights on the windmills that were all flashing in unison. Trying to see outside in the darkness, I needed to turn the lights down in my cockpit, so I turned off my navigation system. All I need now was to keep those windmill lights in the same place in the windshield. I have done this many times before using only the stars to navigate. Now I can relax and enjoy the morning. I was thinking how good a cup of coffee would taste, and suddenly the small sliver of the moon went behind the clouds and was gone in a heartbeat. Thinking that I only had to wait for it to get light out, it didn't. It got darker and darker, and I knew immediately this was not good. Time to turn on the landing light and see what was going on. Just what I did not want to see. I was in a snow storm, a full-on blizzard! I was told a long time ago from a wise old pilot, if you are flying at night and don't like what you see, shut the landing lights off. Which is what I did! I got my flashlight out of my pocket and took a look out the window at the wing to make sure there was no ice forming. All was good and nothing to worry about. The outside thermometer read 25° above zero, which was good. The concern is when it is around 32°, the freezing point, that the outside moisture can quickly ice up an airplane and turn it into a falling rock. I turned my navigation equipment back on again to re-check my heading, and confirmed I was still on the way to California.

I have flown in a lot of snow, and it doesn't bother me in the least. But now, having a little light on in my cockpit, I noticed something that did bother me. The oil pressure gauge showed that my brand-new engine was going south faster than I was. It went from 60 PSI down to 30 PSI, then down to zero! No need for coffee anymore. I was now wide awake and alert. Time to do my pilot-thing and get serious. Cross check all gauges and figure out a game plan, and do it quickly. Going down into the darkness and the unknown is not my first plan.

Sweet-talking the engine is, and is now the first on my list of things to do. "Mr. Lycoming, I see we need to talk! If you are leaking oil, or if your oil pump is failing, your oil temperature should be higher than it is." If that were the case, I would start to see a rise in the oil temperature, but it was steady at 155°, right where it was supposed to be. The cockpit is no place to panic. Be calm at all times. You just have to work through your problems. By process of elimination, there is a good chance it is the gauge. "Yes, without a doubt, absolutely 100% sure, it's the gauge. It's just got to be a defective gauge." I kept telling myself that for 45 minutes until the sun came up, and I found an airport to land and inspect everything. I found out it was just the gauge. Of course, it was just the gauge. I was never worried…not for a second!

Top off the fuel tanks, and off into the wild blue yonder again. Now it is time to find some good weather at higher altitude and put some miles behind me. Heading south, I found some high mountains I had to go over. Clear skies with some light winds looked good to me. I climbed to 9,500 feet, a safe altitude over the mountains. Looking to the west off my right wing, I could see the storms along the coast. As I flew alongside the storm, I could see the tops of the clouds. They were a lot higher than I could go, and it made me glad I didn't have to go through that storm. My flight path was clear. Nothing to do but settle in for a nice ride and enjoy the scenery.

Ouch! Without warning, I flew right through some clear-air turbulence. Everything in the cockpit went up, including me. I hit my head on a steel reinforcing channel above me in the cockpit. I was sure I cut my head and was bleeding, but no, it seemed like I was okay. I did not see that coming. But I should have known, flying next to a storm that has turbulence and wind, can extend way outside the storm. This was a stupid mistake. I should have tightened my seatbelt and been ready for it. If I were to have been knocked out, even for just a few minutes, I could have died somewhere in the mountains, and no one would have ever known why. Lesson learned, make sure your seatbelt is tight enough to be functional.

And now into the Los Angeles flight control zones. It does get a little busy. It's easy, and you need to pay attention to the air traffic controller. It's just like being married, you just need to do as you are told and you will be just fine. They handed me off from one controller to the next until I got to my destination. Simple.

Once on the ground all I needed to do was find the owner of the aircraft. Not as easy as you would think since it was a big airport. I arrived earlier than he expected, and he was not there yet. The airplane and I were found a short time later, and we tucked the airplane into its new hanger with 25 minutes of daylight to spare. Another easy trip completed.

I love it when a plan comes together!

Chapter 19

Chasing the Breezy

Sanford has a lot of time and experience in many single-engine aircraft. While he always says you love the one you're with, I see his face light up when he talks about two airplanes – our own beautiful Cessna 170, and the Super Breezy. With all his time and experience flying the Super Breezy, Sanford was recruited to test fly and deliver a Breezy. The Breezy's have much the same style and flying characteristics, and this one had a smaller engine while sporting unique flight controls and a fuselage style that made it light and nimble.

Each Breezy is unique, but this one is even more so. Beautiful hand-finished wood trim, custom and comfortable leather seats, and a steering wheel at the controls, are just some of the items that make this airplane one to cherish and remember.

This airplane had an unfortunate start in its life since her maiden voyage did not turn out so well. Some damage to the airplane was done and was brought to Yakima for repairs. It was put in the very-capable hands of a local friend and expert in building one-off and home-built, unique aircraft. He was the builder of the original Super Breezy.

Carefully and completely repairing and restoring the aircraft, the Breezy was now ready to be test flown, again. But they still did not know why the first flight was unsuccessful. Sanford's phone rang, and our local friend and builder asked Sanford to help. He needed Sanford's experience and expertise to diagnose the problem so modifications could be done to make it fly safely. We got out his leather helmet and face mask – yes, the one with the skull on it – and off to the airport to begin his process of inspecting and troubleshooting the airplane.

Following a thorough inspection, along with a discussion with our friend/expert who rebuilt the airplane, Sanford is ready for the next step of the process. Slow to progressively-fast taxiing the airplane while staying on the ground to get a feel for the flight controls and make sure it tracks straight. Sanford memorizes the location of the controls and switches since he cannot see them under his seat. He dons the mask and leather helmet, fitted with his aviation headset, and climbs aboard. He starts the engine and does a run-up to make sure it is running smoothly. Ready to taxi, Sanford radios the control tower and advises he will only be doing slow to fast taxi runs to test the airplane, remaining on the ground. The control tower grants permission, and Sanford is ready to start the first test run.

Now rolling down the runway, slowly at first, all seems good. The Breezy handles well on the ground, tracks straight, and the controls feel normal. More power, and all the same result. More power now, and things don't seem right. The airplane should be near the point of feeling light and taking flight, but it is still firmly on the ground. A little more power, while pulling the controls for the elevator back to raise the nose, gives the same result: Still firmly on the ground. More power, more elevator back to raise the nose, trying to determine if the airplane is not balanced correctly, and suddenly Sanford is in full flight. Not what he intended to do yet!

The elevator of the airplane is situated at the very back on the tail. It controls the attitude of the airplane to make it pitch up or pitch down. Pull the controls back, and the airplane pitches up. Push the controls forward, and it pitches down. The preferred landing attitude of this airplane is with the nose up, allowing the main wheels to touch down first.

With the elevator controls fully pulled back, Sanford is flying in a completely flat attitude. He cannot raise the nose any further with the controls to land the airplane. If he relaxes the controls, the nose will pitch down and the nose wheel would hit first, and the airplane would instantly be out of control. He is only a few feet in the air but in a very dangerous situation and quickly running out of runway. His only way to get back on the ground is to reduce power. If he reduces too much power, he would lose the force that the wind already has on the elevator, and would cause the nose to pitch down.

Sanford eases the power back and feels the airplane descending in a flat configuration. Waiting for his speed to gradually diminish, he touches down in a three-point landing and is able to stop while still on the runway. Sanford calls the tower, requests to slowly taxi back to the hangar, and is quickly granted permission.

By the time he reached the hangar, Sanford had already figured out the problem. With a level (actually his iPhone and an app), he could see the horizontal stabilizer, the tail section that holds the elevator assembly, is not level with the wings. The front of the horizontal stabilizer is pitched up instead of flat. This caused the wind to get under the tail section, hitting the bottom surface, and pushing the tail up / nose down. This cancelled out the work the elevator was trying to do, to push the tail down / nose up.

The building plans for the airplane had been modified with a spacer inserted to slightly raise the front of the horizontal stabilizer. It was just enough to make the airplane unstable, and most likely the reason the first attempt at flight was unsuccessful. The airplane was repaired and returned to original specifications. All else had checked out during Sanford's fast-taxi experience, so an attempt to make a full, controlled flight was next. It went well. Problem solved. Problem number one, that is.

There were four more major problems on this airplane that Sanford skillfully handled, even some in flight, that some pilots may not have survived. I swear, this airplane tried to kill Sanford five times.

Final flight testing is complete, the airplane is flying great, and the engine is running well. The Breezy is ready to make her flight to her new home just outside St. Louis, Missouri. And of course, Sanford would fly it there. He was confident the major issues were all found and fixed, although he was still worried that there may be some further issues during the trip. It could be difficult for Sanford to get help if he has to land the airplane off-airport. On top of that, long and consecutive days of flying a Breezy takes a physical toll on Sanford.

We decided it would be a good idea to have ground support all along his travel route. Sanford would be flying close to Interstate 90 the majority of the way, so a chase car was the answer. Ground transportation would be available if needed, plus handle the logistics of food, water, and hotels. The Breezy flies comfortably around 70 to 80 mph, matched perfectly with a car on the freeway. Sanford didn't even have to ask; I am always ready for a road trip!

We arrived in Missoula, Montana, late in the afternoon on day one. We had warm weather and clear blue skies and a nice tail wind for most of the ride. Over the Idaho mountains, between Coeur d'Alene and into Missoula, Sanford had his hands full with the turbulence through the mountain passes. He says it was like holding on to a bucking bronco. You grab and hang onto anything that is attached. And as you can see from the picture, there is not much within reach!

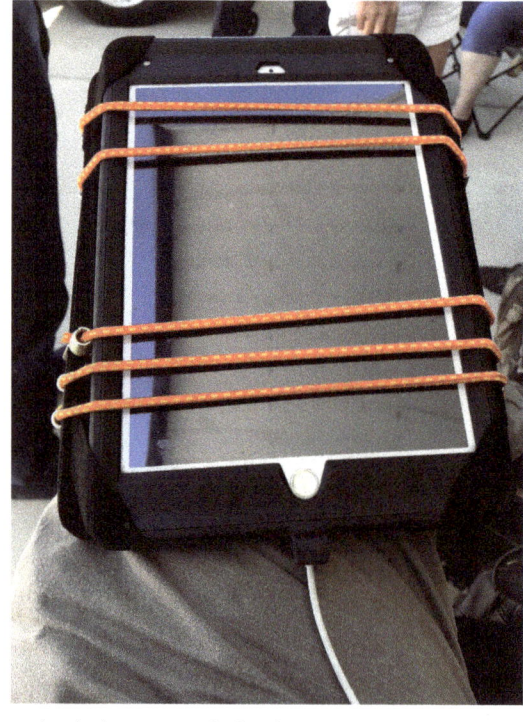

With no navigational equipment on the airplane, the only thing Sanford had was his iPad. He attached the iPad on top of his thigh using a kneeboard that came with one wide elastic strap that fastened with velcro. And just for insurance, he decided to strap one small bungee cord around the iPad and his leg. While going through the Idaho mountain turbulence, he noticed the elastic strap was slapping the bottom of his leg. When Sanford reached down to feel what was going on, he discovered the strap holding his kneeboard and iPad was starting to come loose. While trying to maintain control of the airplane in the turbulence, he had to take his hands off the controls and quickly tie a knot in the strap so he would not lose his iPad. At his next fuel stop at an airport, Sanford attached ten small bungee cords around the iPad and his leg. He would have put more on, but that's all he had left. There were two more but they were in use, around his ankles, holding his pant legs down in the wind. He was confident it was now secure, but he did turn on the security code on the iPad, just in case someone found it!

Day two's travels brought us to Sheridan, Wyoming. It was a long day for Sanford with nearly eight hours of flying and three fuel stops in-between Missoula and Sheridan. I usually fueled the car on the same stops as Sanford, but I thought I could skip one and be okay. Unfortunately, that was not the case, so at one point I had to pull off the interstate and get gas. I thought I could catch up with him rather quickly since the speed limit in Montana was 80 mph. Little did I know he caught a tail wind and was actually going faster than me, plus he cheated and cut the corners!

Before we got started that morning, we had to purchase another hand-held aircraft radio. Our charger went out, and I could not recharge the radio. It was our only communication while Sanford was in flight, and it was important we have it. These radios are not available in standard electronics stores, so you either have to order them or buy them at an airport. But it was Sunday. And this is why I love the aviation industry. There was an avionics shop at the Missoula airport with an after-hours emergency number. Sanford called Saturday evening and left a message, and the owner responded Sunday morning. He was willing to come in and open his shop and sold us another hand-held radio. On top of that, he found the problem with our old charger and gave us a new one – at no charge. Did I mention how much I love the aviation industry and its people?

One of Sanford's fuel stops on day two was in Butte, Montana. After he landed, the lineman marshalled him in to park and get fuel. After

Sanford shut the engine down, the first thing the lineman said was: "Do you people have a death wish? You guys must be crazy. I saw only one other guy fly one of these airplanes." Sanford asked him if it was a few years ago and was it yellow. The lineman responded yes. Sanford said, with a grin: "That was me."

While flying across Montana, Sanford told me about two herds of elk that were just out of sight from the highway. The bull elk were all laying together and looked content and proud. About three blocks away were cows and their new calves. For some reason, they do not mingle at that time of year, but stay close for safety. The antelope were plentiful too, and when Sanford flew over them, they did not run. They only gazed up and looked at Sanford with the expression on their face of, what the heck is that?

When Sanford finished day two, landing at Sheridan, two linemen came out to greet and marshal him in. After he shut the aircraft down and took off his leather helmet, headset, electronics, and all ten bungee cords attached to his leg, the gentlemen asked: "What are you doing on this. Are you crazy?" There's that word again, crazy! Then they asked Sanford what could they help him with. He asked them to help him get off the airplane because his legs and joints were so stiff from the wind and weather. And they did. The airplane needed to be pushed into the hangar for the night, and the linemen helped with that also. As they approached the airplane, they had a confused look on their face and asked how they should steer the airplane. Sanford told him to stand in front of the airplane and walk backwards, pull the airplane into the hangar, while using their hands on the rudder pedals to steer. Then he added: "Just don't get run over by the nose wheel while walking backwards!"

Early in the morning on day three, we left the hotel and made our way to the Sheridan airport for another day's travel. Sanford sent me on the way to Interstate 90 right away since I had to work my way through town. While I argued with my iPhone and the ever-changing driving directions, Sanford finished pre-flighting the airplane, taking special precautions that everything was securely strapped down. He had to securely strap himself down too, and attach everything he needed to his body, which included plugging the iPad into the charger. Then Sanford carefully secured the iPad to his thigh, with all ten bungee cords, secured his pant legs with the two remaining bungee cords, secured the seatbelt with one click, and secured the headset cord inside his coat so it would not flop around in the wind. Next his safety glasses, which act as a windshield, and then his protective skull mask that goes over his face. Following that it is the leather helmet that goes on over the top of everything, with the headset attached to the helmet, and remembering to snap it securely around his chin. Then the next thing is to pull the face mask out and route the microphone inside it, make sure the foam muff is on, and place it in front of his lips for communication. Turn on the master switch, alternator switch, radio switch, strobe light switch, set the mixture control, push the carburetor heat in, set the throttle, turn on the start key, turn on the magnetos, and finally ready to go. It was quite a list for his starting procedure, so having to do it often was not desirable, especially just a few minutes later.

We use a Spot satellite tracker on all our flights, especially Sanford's deliveries. I can follow him on the internet with live updates every few minutes, and it gives me a lot of peace of mind knowing exactly where he is and how I can find him if he has to make an off-airport landing. On that morning, after going through the entire list of starting procedures, and taking off from the airport, he realized he forgot to turn on the Spot tracker. The next opportunity for him to land was at Johnson County Airport, next to a town called Buffalo, Wyoming. They had a long runway, so he made a short landing, pulled over to the side of the runway, and shut off the engine. It was a small airport and he was only going to be there a few minutes. Sanford unhooked everything and got off the seat so he could get into his suitcase that was strapped in the back seat, with the Spot tracker sitting inside the cover. Sanford turned it on and then returned to the same process of attaching and turning on everything before taking off. About the time he was ready to start the airplane, he looked up to see the airport pickup truck about a quarter of a mile away, racing down the gravel road, with dust in the air. He was discovered! The driver stopped and Sanford gave him a thumbs up. The driver asked if he was okay, and Sanford said yes, that he just had a wardrobe malfunction. Then it was Sanford's turn to catch up to me on the freeway. It didn't take him long, because I'm sure he cut the corners again.

The next flight leg was between Rapid City and Chamberlain, South Dakota. It was a long stretch, so Sanford decided to go direct so he would not have to worry about fuel and fatigue. This allowed me to drive the speed limit, or maybe a little more. There were no airports with fuel, hangars, and overnight services in-between. Overnight hangar availability is zilch in Chamberlain too, unless, of course, you are Sanford, and have gotten to know the local crop duster pilot / airport manager and can get into his private hangar for the night. It is worth saying again, I just love aviation people and the aviation industry.

The crop duster / airport manager told Sanford where we could find the remote door opener, only to discover the batteries were dead, and we had no way of opening the hangar door. In most cases, this would be disastrous, but not for aviation people Sanford has gotten to know. He made a phone call to the crop duster, who was actually in his airplane spraying a field at the time in Iowa. While flying, the crop duster called a friend, who had a brother, who was available, to come out, and had the combination for the office door of the building, and could open the hangar door from the inside. A short time later, the Breezy was safely tucked in the hangar for the night. And the brother of the friend of the crop duster came out the next morning to unlock the hangar. Coincidentally, Sanford first met the crop duster / airport manager a few years earlier when he was delivering the first Super Breezy.

With me in charge of logistics, I had made a reservation at a local hotel in Chamberlain. We drove there, dropped off our luggage, and headed to a restaurant Sanford told me about some time ago. This restaurant had special meaning since he stopped there while on the first Super Breezy trip. He was traveling alone on that trip and arrived at the restaurant very tired, very dehydrated, and very hungry. He got a wonderful meal, sent compliments to the cook, and then got to meet the cook, who was the owner. On this Breezy trip, I had the honor of meeting the owner as well. She remembered Sanford and was very excited to see him again. We also met a wonderful family from New York who were on vacation driving to Yellowstone National Park.

Day four started out with a crowd at the airport to watch Sanford take off with the Breezy. The airplane is definitely unique, and it always gathers people and brings smiles. The owner of the restaurant and her husband were there, and well as the family from New York we had met at the restaurant the night before. I think there were some other people there as well, most likely who were also at the restaurant and heard us talking about our trip. We pulled the airplane over and got some fuel while everyone took pictures. Sanford went through the long sequence of hooking everything onto his body again, including ALL the bungee cords, said our goodbyes, and headed eastbound with the well wishes of all our new friends.

Our next stop was Sioux Falls, South Dakota. When Sanford was getting within radio range of the airport control tower, he noticed the foam cover for the microphone of his headset had come off. Still inside his face mask, it found its way to his upper lip below his nose. Sanford knew he better not lose the foam cover, or he would not be able to communicate clearly since it eliminates wind noise. Then he felt it slide over to his left cheek as it was working its way out of the mask! Sanford quickly put his left hand on top of it to trap it, took his right knee and put it against the control wheel to hold the airplane steady, while using his right hand to grab the foam muff. He unzipped his coat with his left hand, and put the muff in an inside pocket in his shirt for safe keeping. Communication is a very serious thing in an airport environment such as Sioux Falls. Now Sanford was close enough and needed to call the control tower. "Sioux Falls Tower, November Five Five Three Bravo Bravo, seven miles to the west with information Alpha, landing." The tower responded: "Five Five Three Bravo Bravo say again." Sanford repeated that he was inbound for landing while holding his hand over the mask to try and block the wind. The tower responded: "Having a hard time understanding you. Are you landing?" Sanford said: "Affirmative." The controller instructed him to enter a left downwind for Runway 3-3 and that he was clear to land, which Sanford acknowledged.

After Sanford fueled the airplane and went inside the office to take a short break and stretch his aching legs, two people from the FAA Control Tower came walking in, looking for Sanford. They said: "Is that your aircraft?" Sanford asked what he did wrong, knowing a visit from the control tower is never good and expecting they have something to say about the communication problem. They told Sanford he did nothing wrong, but that they wanted to look at the airplane, and said it was 'really cool'. One gentleman said he was the guy in the tower Sanford was talking with, and that he couldn't figure out why it was so hard to understand Sanford. The controller got the binoculars out to see what Sanford was flying, and said he just had to come down and take a look at this unique aircraft. Sanford offered to let the controllers sit on the airplane and he would take their picture. They were thrilled and all smiles! They were extremely nice people and Sanford enjoyed answering their questions. It is too bad they rarely get a chance to come out and visit with pilots. I think they should do it more often.

After the break, it was eastbound again. The plan was Albert Lea, Minnesota, for that night, so we pressed on knowing Sanford was guaranteed a hangar at the airport. He was born and raised in Albert Lea and started his aviation career there. It is always nice to stop there since we are surrounded by many family and friends. As soon as we arrived, we grabbed a bucket of soapy water and went to cleaning the entire airplane since we expected to make our final destination the next day. It was a long flight so far, and many, many bugs met their demise along the way.

Day five and we were at a turning point. Our travel route would depart Interstate 90 at Albert Lea and head southeast toward St. Louis, Missouri. Our final destination was just east of St. Louis in Greenville, just across the border in Illinois.

That morning, like every other morning, we hit the floor running. A quick snack for breakfast then out to the airport. There were already people waiting for us so they could see the Breezy and watch Sanford take off. He checked the weather on the way to the airport and saw storms were coming in, so we had to get going quickly to stay ahead of it. Storm fronts had chased us all the way across from the west coast, and we needed to stay ahead of them. I dropped Sanford off at the airport, before they were even open, and started driving. Once open, he was able to fuel the airplane, pre-flight it, and say his good-byes to everyone. He then took a direct course from Albert Lea to Greenville, while I zigged and zagged across Iowa and Illinois. The forecast also called for headwinds in northern Iowa, which actually turned out to be a light tail wind the entire way. Have you ever noticed the weather forecast is wrong, a lot? Don't you wish we could be wrong a lot and still get paid for your job? Just a thought.

The final flight leg was just over three hours to the Breezy's new home. After two hours, Sanford was well ahead of me so he decided to land to stretch his legs at an airport in Iowa. He called me and found out my iPhone, who is now my new best friend, had re-routed me on a faster route, and I was only an hour behind. Sanford's break got cut short and he had to strap onto the flying machine again. It was a welcome sight when Greenville came into his view. Sanford said it was one of the prettiest airports he had ever seen, with dark green mowed grass surrounded by healthy, thick corn and soy bean fields. As he set up for his landing sequence, he heard a welcoming voice on the radio, saying: "Can you hear me Breezy!" Sanford says he loves it when a plan comes together, as we both arrived at the airport at the same time. Once on the ground, Sanford could see a crowd of people waiting for him, as though they knew he was coming.

They directed Sanford to taxi the Breezy to the owner's hangar and told him he would arrive in 15 minutes. Everyone there to watch his arrival was given a rag and cleaner and told to hurry up and clean the bugs off this man's brand-new airplane! After the owner did a walk-around with Sanford, the next order of business was a checkout flight in the airplane. Sanford moved to the back seat for the first time and handed off the keys to her proud, and smiling, owner. Sanford truly enjoyed watching someone else fly this exciting airplane.

This was the route we took from Yakima, Washington, to Greenville, Illinois over five days.

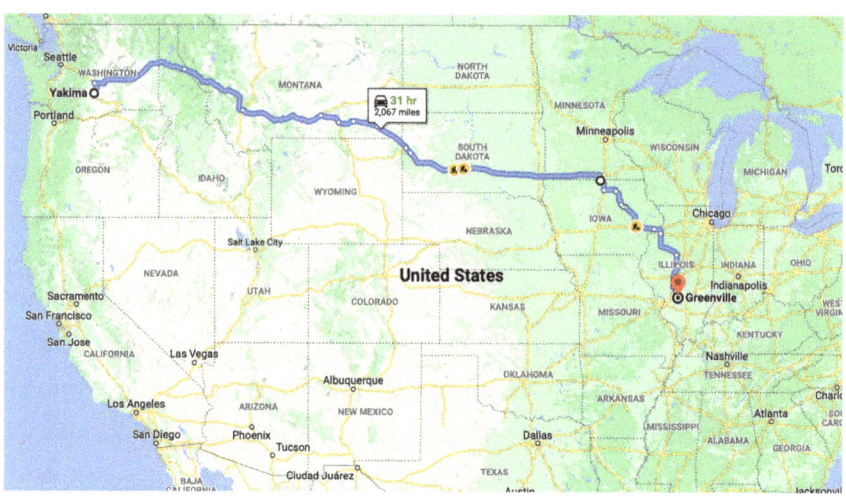

Sanford had a lot of fun on this trip, telling people at the airports he has cars following him. He claims the airplane must be a chick magnet, because every time he lands, women show up. Every time, right on cue, a car would pull up, I would get out, and walk into the conversation. All I can say is Sanford is lucky I was always the first <u>and</u> last chick to show up! And actually, he does get cars following him. There have been times when I had to work my way through traffic to maintain speed with him because there was a cluster of cars driving at the same speed, watching him for several miles. I'm happy that some people recognized and enjoyed watching such a fun and unique airplane.

Chapter 20

Chasing the Breezy – After the Show

After delivering the Breezy to Illinois, we arrived home on a very nice, and quick, commercial flight. We are still basking in the success of delivering such a unique and exceptional new airplane to her owner. It is bitter-sweet because of the excitement of making such a cross-country trip, and then letting go of the airplane that Sanford came to know and 'wear' and trust. I truly believe each airplane has their own personality, heart, and soul, and I am happy the Breezy carried Sanford safe and sound to her new home.

Here are some interesting facts about the Breezy:

- It is an airplane in all the basic ways, so it will fly at altitudes expected of other single-engine aircraft. Sanford flew the Breezy (and previous Breezy's) at altitudes that offered the best temperatures for his comfort. Higher altitudes offer cooler temperatures, and lower altitudes are warmer. But if the altitude range isn't enough, Sanford uses his 'ground-adjustable thermostat'. In other words, land and either take off or put on more clothes!

- The airplane holds 40 gallons of fuel. It burns an average of about five gallons an hour. This would calculate to eight hours of flying, but pilots always keep about an hour of fuel in case they need to deviate to another airport than they originally planned on to get fuel.

- The Breezy flies comfortably between 50 and 75 mph. Landing speed at touchdown is about 40 mph. While performing the flight testing, Sanford has taken it to just over 100 mph for testing purposes only.

- Clear days and light winds are optimum days to fly. With the airplane's instruments completely exposed, as well as the pilot, flying in rain is not an option. It can fly on windy days, although it is not as much fun as a calm day. Turbulence makes for a difficult and exhausting ride, much like Sanford experienced when he traveled through the mountains of Washington, Idaho, and Montana.

- The airplane carries two people, sitting one in front of the other. The advantage of being a passenger on the Breezy is the pilot blocks about 70% of the wind, so the ride in the back seat is really nice!

- The engine is a 150 hp Lycoming and air cooled. The Breezy's owner proudly built the engine, which Sanford says is one of the smoothest and best running engines he has flown. On a standard aircraft with the engine in the front, the down-thrust blade has more power than the up-thrust, causing the aircraft to turn to the left on takeoff. This is called P-Factor. The configuration of this Breezy has the engine mounted behind the pilot, pointing backwards, which instead causes the airplane to turn to the right on takeoff. This requires an unnatural reaction from the pilot to keep it straight down the runway while accelerating. This Breezy also sports a beautiful wooden prop.

- The Breezy is an experimental airplane built from plans, so each one is unique and considered a 'one-off'. The very first one was designed and constructed in 1964 with a 90 hp engine.

- The pilot and passenger cannot have any loose items during flight. With the engine behind the pilot, anything that might come loose would instantly go through and hit the propeller, causing major damage and would most likely cause full loss of power.

We had stunning weather for the entire Breezy trip. As Sanford planned and forecasted, we travelled in a high-pressure bubble, moving with it across the states. It was important that we kept moving at the same pace to stay in the beautiful weather. It nearly caught up to us in Minnesota and Iowa. Early in the afternoon on day five, just a few hours after we left Albert Lea, Minnesota, storms rolled through Iowa with high winds, thunderstorms, rain, and 1-inch hail.

All in all, Sanford flew nearly 29 hours from Yakima to Greenville in five days, figuring he averaged around 75 mph. I drove about 2,100 miles over the course of the trip while leading, chasing, following, finding, dodging, and avoiding. Dodging construction barricades, and avoiding speeding tickets. As it turned out, it was speed-awareness day in Illinois as I drove through and luckily I did not enjoy a personal encounter with Illinois' finest!

Truly, the best part about the entire trip was all of the wonderful people we met along the way. Sanford has always shared with me his stories about who and how he has met some very memorable people that we are proud to now call friends. He has always said he would like to share the actual experience with me, and I was fortunate to have that chance. Most likely a chance of a lifetime.

Chapter 21

WHERE THERE'S SMOKE, THERE'S FIRE...AND A RAVEN

Of all the delivery trips that I have gotten to ride along with Sanford, this trip held pure excitement from one end of the spectrum to the other. This is my day-by-day account of the trip from the back seat of a great Super Cub.

Tuesday:

Sanford and I have enjoyed a few days with wonderful friends in the Anchorage area. This trip was supposed to be a vacation, one where we flew our own airplane from Yakima to Anchorage for a week's vacation. We planned to take a few days and do some fly-outs with two other airplanes and friends, but things change.

As it turns out, we flew up last Saturday commercially, and tomorrow we are hoping to depart with another delivery airplane from Lake Hood strip near Anchorage to Yakima. Just a coincidence, but at the last minute, Sanford was recruited and hired to return a great Alaskan Super Cub to Yakima for its owner. We decided to combine work and play, but isn't that how it always goes?

Weather providing, which has been questionable the last few days, we hope to be off at first light tomorrow morning. If all goes well, it will be three long days to return to Yakima with the Super Cub.

Wednesday:

Rain and layers of low clouds started our morning. We knew better weather was ahead so Sanford decided to make a run at it. We had to get through two passes called Sheep Mountain Pass and Tahneta Pass, and got through with no problem. As they say, timing is everything.

We always enjoy seeing the Alaskan pipeline along the way and marvel at its engineering. Sections are above ground because of permafrost and zig zag to allow for expansion due to the extreme hot and cold temperature swings in this region. We cannot help but think about all the people that worked so hard on this massive project for so many years.

Even with the rainy and cloudy weather, Alaska holds a beauty unlike anything else. In fact, flying at lower altitudes offers better wildlife viewing. We could not count the mountain goats we saw today, their coats completely white and kids running with the herds. I saw a black elk for the first time, along with a black bear and many moose, including a cow and a calf. And the ultimate Alaska trophy, the brown bear, better known as the grizzly. Sanford spotted two on a mountain slope at about the 6,000-foot level, and it  looked like a sow and her very large cub. The cub was a dark brown and the sow was a much lighter grey. While mama was a bit concerned about the airplane, cubby just wanted to play and romp around. What a sight!

 Sanford flew me through his favorite spot today in Alaska, called Bear Lakes. It is probably the most beautiful chain of lakes we have ever seen. The waters are crystal clear, enough to see the bottom all the way through each lake. The bonus is that this area holds bison, and we were not disappointed. Several small herds were in the area and kind enough to give us some great photo ops.

But I am going to digress a bit. Our first fuel stop this morning was in Tok, Alaska. We made it just in time to grab some breakfast at Fast Eddie's restaurant across the highway from the airport. After we landed and had just parked the Super Cub, a very large raven landed on the left-wing tip to say good morning. I walked around to that side of the airplane, thinking I needed to shoo him off the wing, but something amazing happened. The raven was unafraid and made eye contact with me. And as I walked closer, instead of flying off, he looked at me as if to say good to see you again. It felt like our Guardian Angels were with us. We could not have asked for a better wing man than this.

We arrived tonight in Whitehorse, Yukon Territory. We parked the Super Cub and tied it down, and got a taxi to the hotel. After checking in, we encountered a gentleman from Russia that asked us if we were also from Russia, since we were carrying a bottle of vodka. It is so much fun to travel and meet people from around the world, and all because we had a bottle of vodka in the elevator!

We will turn more to the south tomorrow as we work our way through the Yukon and into British Columbia, Canada.

Thursday:

We woke up in Whitehorse, Yukon Territory, this morning to blue skies and favorable winds. First item on the agenda was to get some breakfast before we left. We walked across the street from our hotel to a restaurant we have been to before. Great food, way too much, and the funniest waitress I think I have ever met. She was telling us a story about driving to Anchorage and was stopped by an Alaska state trooper. He wrote her a warning ticket because she had only one license plate, the rear plate. The waitress tried to explain to the officer that the Yukon only gives them one license plate. The officer apparently became a little agitated, and reminded her he was only writing her a warning. She said: "Wait, you don't understand. Our Yukon jail only holds 79 inmates, and they don't have enough time to make two plates for every car!" After a phone call to headquarters, the officer apologized and rescinded the warning ticket. She made my day!

In the smaller ponds that we see along the way, there is usually a pair of white swans. I have seen them before, earlier in the spring, but I was pleased to see that they are now swimming with their grey youngling's. Typically, we see only one pair per pond, but in the bigger lakes we will sometimes see more. They are beautiful and huge!

Our first fuel stop today was in Watson Lake, Yukon Territory. This leg of the trip is beautiful because of the vastness of the mountains. They are lush and green and go on forever in all directions. Flying along today, there were many times we wish we had our gold pans with us so we could drop in and try a test pan. This airplane is outfitted with 31-inch Alaskan bush tires that are capable of landing on almost any terrain, so it was tempting. We did see a couple of very remote gold mining operations. Surely there is gold in them thar hills!

After fueling at the historical Watson Lake airport, that was used by the U.S. government in the Cold War, we headed south on an aviation route called the Trench. It is more than a four-hour flight in the Super Cub. Within 20 minutes, we encountered the first of hundreds of forest fires. I understand they have declared western British Columbia a disaster area. The smoke was so thick we could only see the sun in the windshield directly above and in front of us, at 12 o'clock high. We climbed up through it until we got to an altitude of 11,500 feet, finally putting us above the smoke.

Then another complication. The engine on this Super Cub consumed oil at a higher rate than normal. With the four-plus hours of flying through the Trench, some of the most remote country in North America, Sanford noticed the oil pressure was getting low and engine temperature was increasing. We had already passed the remote airstrips that are scattered along the route and were now flying over the main lake with steep, rough shorelines. We had extra oil along in the airplane, but we found no options to land, and turning around to go back and find a remote airstrip was not an option either, since fuel was tight. We were still 30 minutes out, so Sanford headed directly to the Mackenzie airport, nursing the engine as much as possible to keep it from overheating and shutting down.

We finally landed at Mackenzie, British Columbia, at about 4:30 pm this afternoon. Sanford fueled the airplane, and we pulled it over to a tie-down spot to park for the night. After letting the engine sit for a few minutes, and letting the oil drain down, Sanford checked the dip stick to see how low the level was. It didn't even register! He added several quarts of oil and we hoped for the best the next day. Since there was nothing more we could do, it was time to sit and relax and visit with the good people at the Mackenzie airport.

It is a beautiful, small, logging community with three motels in town. There was nothing going on, especially on a Thursday, so getting a room should not have been a problem, we thought. So now it is 6:00 pm, time to find a room, and sit and relax and put our feet up and have a nice quiet evening. The first motel we came to, no vacancies. The second motel we tried, another sign that said no vacancies. Guess what the third and final motel sign said? That's right, no vacancies.

Panic just set in. The next airport heading south was closed due to the smoke from the forest fires. The following airport heading south was too far to make it before dark. It was now looking like our only option was to camp at the airport office tonight! The miracle worker at the airport, who has become a good friend, and who takes care of all of the pilots, even those who forget to cancel their flight plans, came through again. I don't know what we would do without her!

As she and Sanford were driving to her house to pick up the portable bed that she offered to us for the airport office floor, they drove past a logging camp. Mackenzie is a logging community and they have hundreds of workers staying at this camp. Yep, you're right, they left the light on for us!

The camp is built with modular trailers that are attached in rows, some are common areas like the cafeteria and recreation area, and others are for sleeping and showers and bathrooms. Not only were we lucky enough to get a room, it included wonderful people and great food! We are eating like Paul Bunyan tonight because they have a huge cafeteria that feeds all of the loggers, and they fed us a great supper and promised an amazing breakfast in the morning. It is also within walking distance from the airport so a great place for pilots to spend the night.

The camp can hold up to 400 people, and has been here for 25 years. It is used by loggers, construction workers, fire fighters, and the wayward pilot and wife! We discovered the reason the town is so full, is because they evacuated a nearby town due to the fires. And it is heading this way. They are expecting to begin housing evacuees at the camp as well. Prayers to this wonderful community as they brace for this. Thank you to the wonderful people of Mackenzie for the warm and welcoming hospitality. We'll be back!

Saturday:

Good morning all. We are home safe and sound, arriving about 6:00 pm last night. After making our apologies to our beloved kitty about being gone so long, we unloaded the airplane and decided to take the night off. Our adrenaline was still running strong, as we had quite a day of flying yesterday to get home. The complications of flying in the limited visibility, and sometimes zero visibility, due to the forest fire smoke takes its toll on Sanford. There were times it took total concentration and we invoked the 'sterile cockpit' rule: No talking unless there was a problem. It is hard to describe the conditions we flew in, but I'll give it my best. Just like Sanford did yesterday to get us home safe.

We departed Mackenzie yesterday morning, knowing the fires were building and visibility was going to deteriorate throughout the day. Time was of the essence. We gave hugs and said our goodbyes to our wonderful friends at the airport and the logging camp. A couple of hours south is Prince George, British Columbia, which is probably in the worst of the path of the fires. We knew the visibility was bad, but had no idea what we would encounter.

We climbed to 6,000 feet initially to clear the smoke, only to continue to climb to 8,000 feet as the smoke built higher. Getting closer to Prince George, there was a second layer of smoke, much too high for us to climb over. But there was a clear layer in-between that was just high enough for our little Super Cub. We could see many miles between the layers, with a very dark band far ahead and directly in our flight path. We continued on and flew into the gap between the smoke clouds with smooth air and a bit of a tailwind. About 50 miles in, about a 30-minute time period, we were closing in on the dark band where the clouds of smoke joined. It continued to get darker to the point that it was completely black in the cockpit, except for the glow of Sanford's iPad. Good thing, because it illuminated the gauges on the dash so he could monitor the engine and altitude.

We noticed that we now had an orange glow below us outside the airplane. The fires were raging so bad the clouds glowed all around us. We could see straight down through the smoke to the town of Prince George. We knew it was the city because we could see cars with headlights on, street lights were on, parking lot lights were on. The city was dark as night and it was 10:00 am.

Sanford knew we had to press on heading south. The intensity of the fires continued to build through British Columbia, and the smoke closed in behind us. Returning to Mackenzie was not an option since they were now in the thick smoke as well. The orange glow confirmed we were over the major fire, which was not a good place to be in a paper airplane full of 100-octane fuel.

The next airport, another two hours ahead of us, still had pretty good visibility. The wind was blowing the smoke from west to east, so we knew continuing to head south would be the shortest lateral distance to get through the smoke cloud. After going over Prince George, the orange glow dissipated and it began to get brighter. We eventually flew out of the top layer of smoke but still had a thick layer below us for the rest of the flight. Then the theme song from the movie Jaws started playing in my head. Looking to my left and behind us, from where we had just flown through, we could see the very top of a mountain poking above the smoke that looked like a shark fin. That reminded us what was lurking beneath the sea of smoke. Talk about shark-infested waters!

Our destination airport was Kamloops, British Columbia, which was a four-hour flight from Mackenzie. All the airports in-between were closed down due to visibility, and Kamloops was getting worse as well. There is high terrain around the area, so coming down from altitude through the smoke was dicey. Sanford knew of a lake that was up river from the Kamloops airport and clear of their control zone. From the lake, we could then fly the river straight to the airport. We headed for the lake, staying at altitude. Once over the lake, Sanford began a precision spiral down until we could make out the shoreline of the lake. He is very familiar with this area and knew we had very high, very steep and narrow mountains surrounding the lake. It had to be exact, and it was.

Once we landed, Sanford walked around the airplane to inspect it, as he does after every flight. He summoned me to the front of the airplane with a strange look on his face. The propeller, normally black, was now grey. It had so much soot from  the smoke on it that you could write your name in it. Ever seen dirty and dusty cars that someone traced 'wash me' on the back? The propeller now says 'Hi' with a smiley face.

As we were descending into the airport, the visibility was deteriorating at a rapid rate. We knew we only had a short time if we expected to take off again. We immediately had the airplane fueled, and Sanford did a quick check of the airplane and engine oil, which was okay. While I climbed into the airplane, he went into the office to check the weather, file another flight plan, as well as call U.S. Customs to make an appointment to clear back into the states. From the time Sanford hung up the phone and walked to the airplane, the visibility deteriorated even more and they closed the airport. But he had another trick up his sleeve. It is a called a Special VFR Clearance (VFR - Visual Flight Rules). Sanford requested the clearance and the control tower immediately granted it. We departed eastbound over the river, climbing to a safe altitude where we were clear of the mountains on each side of us and could turn south again.

A quick stop at Oroville, Washington, to clear customs and we were headed home. It was much like a horse going back to the barn. Visibility improved immensely to about 10-12 miles, and we were raving about what a beautiful day it was! Our experience earlier in the day gave us a different perspective of good flying weather!

Once home, as always, Sanford checked the airplane and engine oil. Much to his surprise, the engine had not used one drop since we left Mackenzie nearly eight hours before. When we were flying through the Trench, the engine used nearly five quarts of oil in four hours. All of a sudden, it was not using oil nearly at all. Best Sanford can figure is that ash from the forest fires got into the engine while we were flying through it. It must have acted like very, very fine sand paper and etched the inside of the cylinders, allowing the rings to fully seat and seal, drastically lowering the oil consumption rate. If any airplane owners out there have high oil consumption problems with your airplanes, we would <u>not</u> recommend fixing it this way!

Sanford has test flown between 250 and 300 airplanes for their maiden flights. Not every airplane was perfect, and that is why they have someone do the test flight before it is delivered to the customer. People call Sanford to have their airplanes repositioned around the country because of circumstances of various natures, or where they do not feel comfortable or safe to do it themselves.

Sometimes when Sanford makes these deliveries, the weather conditions are less than desirable. He has learned how to deal with bad weather and works the problem safely. He tells other pilots sometimes: "I am going to take off, but do not follow me." This was another one of those trips. In other words, please don't try this at home!

Thanks for following us and all the prayers to carry us safely home. And a special thank you to our wingman, the Raven, who helped us fly safely throughout our journey.

As Sanford and I have said so many times, we've done crazier things, it's just been a while!

Chapter 22

Bandits on the Run

I write this in a new time of my life – retirement! I recently worked at a job that I loved for over 11 years, and I really had no intention to retire quite yet. But with the current economic times that are beyond everyone's control, my position was eliminated. While I wish it could have been on my terms, I have to admit I was looking for an excuse to retire. So here I am, celebrating that if we want, we can go flying or camping, say on a Tuesday, instead of waiting for the weekend!

My first opportunity to ride along with Sanford on an airplane delivery without work or vacation time restrictions just arrived. He had a double delivery this time with a brand-new airplane to deliver to Florida, and then pick up another one at the same airport and deliver it to Wisconsin. It is usually a three- or four-day trip to Florida depending on weather and the time of year. Longer springtime days helped us get there in three. Good thing too, since we were in-between storm fronts all the way across the Lower 48.

We left before sunrise with clouds overhead and beautiful weather to the east. And with Sanford's ability to sniff out tail winds, we climbed to altitude and settled in for a speedy trip. The first day found us in Santa Fe, New Mexico, where we spent the first night.

The second day was much the same for most of the day. Late afternoon we had nearly caught up to the storm that was moving east ahead of us, so spending the night in Louisiana would make for an easy day three for the delivery to central Florida. About an hour before we arrived at our destination for the day, Sanford noticed the engine was running rough. In doing a quick check of the ignition system, he discovered that one of the two electronic ignition components had failed, again. This happened to Sanford in the first few days when he was doing the required 40-hour flyoff on this type of new airplane, before departing the area to make the delivery. It had already been repaired at the factory, but it happened again.

Sanford decided to land at a nearby airport to refuel and check in the area for available aviation mechanics. It was a nice small town and airport, but it lacked the services to repair the airplane or store it overnight in a hangar in case the weather turned bad. After a couple of phone calls back to the factory to help find mechanical services, Sanford decided to fly to Monroe, Louisiana, which was a bigger airport and hopefully would offer a mechanic to help us out. As it turned out, they had a wonderful aviation shop that got us in right away and made the repairs. We then pushed the airplane in the hangar and gratefully accepted the loaner car for the night to find a hotel.

While they were working on the airplane, we had noticed a large hangar nearby that had considerable damage from a tornado a couple of weeks earlier. In fact, it made the national news. It looked like they were just beginning to remove the damaged building. Later as we drove out of the airport to find our way to the hotel, we could see the full extent of the tornado damage. The hangar was not only the newest on the airport, it was huge. It housed four private Cessna Citation jets, one of which was brand new.

In looking at all the rubble, only three were visible with one completely buried under the twisted steel. We were told one of the jets completely turned 180° as a steel girder rammed the tail. Another was sitting with its nose in the air because a massive section of the building had landed on its tail section. Needless to say, all four were a complete loss.

As you probably have realized by now, Sanford and I are both very optimistic and love living a full life. We always consider our glass is half full instead of half empty. The bright side of the storm damage to this community is that no one was injured, and the tornado skipped the aviation museum located right next to the airport. The museum displays both civilian and military airplanes inside and outside the building. These irreplaceable pieces of history were completely untouched, and a few hundred yards away, millions of dollars of state-of-the-art jets were totally destroyed.

We woke the next morning to find beautiful weather. We expected a mid-afternoon delivery in Florida so we took off just after sunrise and made our way to the next fuel stop. This was one of Sanford's favorite stops along this route at the Monroe County airport in Alabama. This airport is frequented by training aircraft from the nearby military base. They use it to practice landing sequences and approach and departure patterns. The draw for the military to use this airport is two-fold. One is that it is a quiet area away from the restricted airspace at the military base. The second is that the manager at the airport is quite an entrepreneur. He carries an abundant supply of fuel for the airplanes and food for the pilots! With every fill of the fuel tank, the pilots eat for free. And not just donuts and coffee. I'm talking a full-blown homemade breakfast and lunch every day of the week. And yes, Sanford and I had breakfast there too. And I discovered something new – cheesy grits! Oh my, talk about comfort food!

Back in the air again to make our way into Florida as Sanford was keeping a watchful eye on a storm system that was moving west to east through the middle of the state. It looked like it was trying to cut the state in half. The edge of the storm system was just south of our destination airport. We had hoped it would move out throughout the day, but instead it continued to build as it was being nourished by the warm gulf coast waters. It became more intense, and by late afternoon they were expecting high winds, lightning, and hail. We made a mad dash for the airport before it could move north and just enough to keep us away.

About an hour before we arrived, Sanford heard from the owner of the new airplane. He was not going to be able to meet us at the airport as planned because he was on the south side of the storm and could not fly through it. He made arrangements with the owner of the next airplane that we were picking up, to swap them out and put the brand new one inside the hangar because of the storms. So now Sanford and I have a situation: Two airplanes, one small hangar, and one very large and angry thunderstorm!

We had planned to take a few days off, rent a car, and see some friends in Florida. But in a moment our plans changed. We were responsible for two airplanes and had to keep them both safe. We decided to switch out the airplanes, move our gear from one to the other, and head north away from the storms as quickly as possible. Once it was all done, we had been on the ground in Florida for only about 20 minutes and were now running from the storm at a high rate of fuel consumption! We weren't sure exactly where, but somewhere in Georgia where the weather was much better. It was late in the day, so we needed to find a place to land and spend the night in the next couple of hours.

Then another call. The owner of the first, new airplane has property in Georgia, about two hours north of where we just took off. He has a grass runway on the property, a house, and a pickup if we need to run to town. We were invited to stay overnight and told where the hidden key was kept. We decided this could be another adventure, and it was! They have over 400 acres of beautifully wooded property in the remote hills of Georgia. We arrived with plenty of daylight to land and get settled, and were met in the cabin by a completely stocked refrigerator and a wonderful place to spend the night.

We were up early and getting ready to continue the second delivery north to Wisconsin. As I was headed to the front door with my suitcase packed, Sanford said I should set it down and come look at something.

He showed me the weather that was ahead of us, and we found ourselves in-between severe weather systems again. Florida was still getting hit with storms, and we had another line of storms about half way between us and Wisconsin. Sanford always says he likes these kinds of decisions because there are no questions. We were not going anywhere for another day.

As a result, we found ourselves in complete isolation, out in the woods, at a beautiful cabin with a huge covered front porch and a porch swing, a hot cup of coffee, and being serenaded by a forest full of birds. The sky was clear, the weather was warm, and we had an entire day to relax and enjoy it all. And we did.

The next morning the storm system in Indiana had nearly moved out of our way so it was time to head north. Sanford planned to modify his flight path and go a little more to the west to skirt around the backside of the storm. While the sky was clear, we were greeted with head winds and quite a bit of rough air. The higher we flew, the stronger the opposing winds were, so we decided to stay low. And if we skirted too close to the storm system, the turbulence increased considerably. Time to buckle up, buttercup!

What a fun flight! We could see everything on the ground, and I lost count of the wild turkeys we saw the entire trip. Late in the day, as we approached our destination in Wisconsin, we were paralleling a highway that ran north and south. It was chilly, so the couple we saw riding a Harley motorcycle seemed out of place. Then Sanford noticed they were keeping up with us in the airplane. Sanford dropped down a bit more and moved closer to the highway where we could get a better look. As he came down in altitude, we gained some speed and were now doing over 100 mph. The couple saw us, waived, and sped up to keep up with us. We were being paced by a motorcycle! It only lasted a couple of miles due to things called stop signs on the highway. Too bad for them!

We arrived in Wisconsin from Georgia in one day to successfully deliver a second airplane in one trip. Even better than that, we were able to see a good friend and spend some time before heading home. Life is good.

Chapter 23

Red-Neck Flying

From Sanford's collection:

Following the delivery of a new Carbon Cub from Yakima, Washington, to central Florida, I picked up an amphibious airplane, called a Mermaid, for delivery back to Yakima. I was enjoying the thought of having a round trip in private airplanes without the hassle of commercial airlines. The owner of the Mermaid spent the summers in Yakima, and wanted to ride along from Florida.

This is a very unique airplane, and there are very few in the United States. It was built in the Czech Republic, and is in the light-sport aircraft category. It is powered by a small 100 hp engine and is capable of burning both aviation fuel and auto gas. It carries two people in a

side-by-side configuration with a small luggage area just behind the seats. The landing gear is hydraulically run, being retractable for water landings and extended for airport landings.

We wanted to get an early start and departed at the crack of dawn. Within the first 20 minutes, we had a problem. The engine started to run very rough, and I was looking for a place to make an emergency landing. I was hopeful we could make it to an airport where we could get some help. I knew of an engine repair shop not far away, so I decided to head that direction to see how far I could get. About 10 minutes from the airport, the engine began to run smooth again, but I was still cautious. Could it just be old gas from sitting around so long in the fuel tanks? The airplane had been run on regular auto gas, which does not last very long before it starts to break down. We had filled the tanks with fresh aviation fuel just before we left, so maybe the engine had worked its way through the old gas. After several more minutes of circling in the area of the airport, I decided to turn back around and head northwest again. That must have been the answer since the engine ran smooth throughout the rest of the trip. After a full day of flying, we arrived in beautiful Grenada, Mississippi, for the night. What a great place to stop.

The next morning, we decided that we couldn't get very far because of bad weather about 200 miles to the west, directly in our path. Since the weather in Grenada was nice, we decided to stay another day and let the storm system move through. I had not yet had a chance to make a water landing with the Mermaid yet, so we decided to take the airplane for a flight and splash in the lake right next to the airport. We unloaded the rest of our gear so it was as light as possible, and headed for the lake. With a slight breeze, the water looked perfect to make some landings and take offs. However, we quickly discovered the Mermaid did not have enough power to take off with two of us in it! Plus, we also realized were taking on water at a very high rate. We were no longer an airplane, but a sinking ship!

A quick, relaxing flight quickly became a long day at sea. I had to taxi the airplane at full throttle and took a direct course to the closest shore. As we came into shallow water, I put the landing gear down under the airplane so it would not hit bottom and damage the hull. With the engine over-heating, and the airplane sinking lower in the water all the time, we barely made it to shore.

Now we had to figure out how we were going to get back to the airport. There were boats competing in a fishing tournament, but none were interested in coming to our aid. While we waited and kept trying to flag down a boat, we were bailing the water out of the airplane in hopes we could fly it out. I had also called a friend that lived in Grenada to see if he could find us some help. He was a local farmer that I had met just a week before, and had a huge operation that grew hundreds and hundreds of acres of cotton. He said he would call the Park Service and see if they could lend us a hand.

Eventually, a boat arrived, and it was the Park Service patrol boat. They gave us a tow to the nearest boat ramp, and as we came into shallow water again, I put the landing gear down so the airplane would not hit bottom. But we still needed to get the airplane out of the water. My friend had arrived in his pickup, so we decided the best way was to tow the airplane up the boat ramp and drain the water out of it again. After several minutes and an unbelievable amount of water, the airplane was ready to fly again. Trouble was, we were not at an airport.

We decided the owner of the Mermaid would ride along with my friend back to the airport, and I would fly the airplane by myself. We turned the airplane around and pointed it down the boat ramp, I climbed in, started the engine, taxied into the water, retracted the gear, and took off as fast as I could before it sank!

The airplane took off with no problems, and we parked it back at the airport. I quickly decided no more water landings on the trip. A quick pleasure flight turned into the majority of the day wondering if we were going to go down with the ship. Plus, the owner had a very intense conversation about the airplane with the Park rangers. It seems this was a state park reservoir, and airplanes are not allowed to land on the lake without prior permission. After talking with the Park rangers, who were very nice and understanding that we were not from the area, we were given a verbal warning not to do that again. Believe me, we had no intention to!

Once back at the airport we had to do some fixing so we could make the rest of the trip from Mississippi to Washington State. This airplane's engine was equipped with an overflow tank for the engine coolant, and it was mounted too close to the engine. We discovered a non-licensed mechanic had done some modifications and relocated the tank. While taxiing at full power to make it to shore, the heat from the engine melted a hole in the side of the overflow tank. Coolant leaked out onto the hot engine, putting out a cloud of steam, making it look like the engine was smoking. The owner was afraid we had overheated the engine and would ruin it, but I explained we had no choice. It was power taxi to the shoreline for safety, or sink in the middle of the lake.

With limited resources, we decided to do a red-neck fix to seal up the hole. A roll of gorilla tape and some Flex-Seal (as seen on tv), and we were good to go. My farmer friend even guaranteed the fix would hold, at least until Wyoming. We had a good laugh and decided that was enough for one day.

The decision to wait a day for the weather turned out to be a good decision, and we had great flying weather the next couple of days. At the end of our third day of flying, we arrived in Sheridan, Wyoming, and decided to spend the night. In checking our red-neck fix of the overflow tank, we discovered the Mississippi red-neck warranty had expired, finding the gorilla tape and Flex-Seal melted, opening the original hole. This time we pulled the tank completely out of the airplane and cleaned the tape and rubber residue off. We re-patched the hole with a tube of JB Weld and covered it with heat-resistant aluminum tape. The fix successfully lasted until our arrival in Yakima, Washington. Unfortunately, there were other problems yet to surface.

We fueled the airplane and prepared for another day of flying northwest. In trying to depart out of Sheridan, the altitude of the airport was high at 4,000 feet, and the airplane struggled to climb with the two of us on board and full of fuel. By the time we were over the end of the runway, we were only about 100 feet in the air. I had to circle the airport several times, slowly climbing, before we could clear the Big Horn Canyon National Recreational Area, where the mountain tops were over 9,000 feet high.

Once above the mountains, I leveled off and gained airspeed. Then suddenly the airplane started to bang loudly. I pulled the control stick back, slowing the airplane, since I thought we had a structural failure. The noise stopped. I slowly lowered the nose to gain airspeed, and the loud banging started again. I immediately started looking for a place where we could survive a forced landing in the mountains. There was nothing but canyons and cliffs below us. I again slowed the airplane and plotted a course to the nearest airport. I planned for the worst, and hoped for the best.

We managed to land at an airport and inspected the airplane. I found a fairing on the bottom of the wing, that covers the gap between the wing and the fuselage, broke loose. It was flopping in the wind, making the loud banging noise. Another red-neck fix was in order. The maintenance facility at the airport came through with more gorilla tape for us. Problem solved!

As we proceeded into Montana, we were met with poor visibility due to forest fire smoke. We could not go any further that day, and decided to spend the night in Missoula. The next several days were forecast to be the same since there were so many fires burning throughout Montana, Idaho, Washington, and Oregon. After another day of waiting to see if it would clear enough to fly, it did not. We were down to 1-1/4 mile of visibility. Since we still had many miles of mountainous terrain to fly over, we decided to leave the airplane in Missoula and rent a car to drive the rest of the way to Yakima. It would take about a week before the smoke cleared enough to fly the airplane the final leg home.

Smoke gone! Back to work!

As soon as the smoke cleared, the owner and myself drove to Missoula so I could fly the Mermaid home to Yakima. While doing a thorough pre-flight inspection of the airplane, I noticed a broken, leaking hydraulic line that runs the retractable landing gear. Funny thing, when we were getting ready to initially depart from Florida, another pilot, who was not a mechanic, and who was flying and doing some maintenance on the Mermaid, gave me a box of tubing, saying it was just in case we had problems with the hydraulic landing gear leaking. I remember thinking it was odd, but accepted the tubing and stored it in the airplane.

I discovered the hydraulic fluid and the plastic tubing the non-mechanic had used on the landing gear were not compatible. The fluid attacked the plastic tubing, melting it.

Since it was a Sunday, there were limited services at the Missoula airport and no mechanics were available. So, it was up to me to fix the broken hydraulic line. I was on my back, under the front of the airplane, outside on the ramp of the airport, trying to replace the bad tubing. I had my right arm up inside the front wheel compartment, when

I accidentally bumped the over-center rod. It caused the landing gear to retract, and the nose of the airplane fell on me. The clam-shell gear door was still open, vertically up and down, and was trying to cut into my chest. Luckily, I had my phone in my right front shirt pocket, and the landing gear door fell directly on the phone. The owner was close by and heard me yell, and was able to lift the nose of the airplane just enough so that I could trigger the nose gear to extend again. Nothing broken, not even the phone. I'm glad I had an Otter Box cell phone case; it saved my life. I just had the air squeezed out of me, and I ended up with a bruise and a sore chest for about a week.

With the hydraulic line replaced, it is time to get going. I got in the airplane, ready to go, and now it won't start. We've done nothing but red-neck fixes the entire trip, so why change now? I had to use a slotted screwdriver to short-out the starter, and get the engine running. But please don't ask how I knew how to do that!

Finally, back in the air. What could possibly go wrong now? I had already decided to leave the landing gear down after fixing the hydraulic line, just in case it did not hold. At least, I thought, I could count on the gear being down and ready for landing. Just about 20 miles from Yakima, the right main gear light, indicating the gear was down and locked for landing, started to flicker. And then went out. It could only be one of two things: Either the landing gear lost pressure and was no longer locked in place, or the sensor on the switch was bad and caused the light to go out. For the second time this trip, I planned for the worst and hoped for the best. I got lucky, again, and it was just the sensor. But I did one of the most perfect, soft landings in my life!

The airplane eventually underwent some major repairs while in Yakima, and was restored to good flying condition. The owner sold the airplane, and I heard it was going to be transported south, out of the United States. To no one's surprise, I had no desire to deliver the airplane to its new home!

Time goes by, and Diane and I sell our house in Yakima and move to Fort Myers, Florida, where we have been enjoying a whole new style of flying and retirement living. On one of our day-trips to a nearby airport, I couldn't believe what I saw. Here was the Mermaid, the very same airplane, tied down on the ramp!

I haven't been back to that airport since.

Chapter 24

SURPRISE, SURPRISE

From Sanford's collection:

Just when I thought things were going well, and I had done something really special for a good friend, something very scary happened. I was nearly arrested.

My good friend was working as a tour boat captain on the Columbia River in Washington State. He is also a pilot, an internationally-trained master chef, amongst many other impressive things, and we instantly became good friends. He had relocated from the east coast while his mother and sisters remained in the Boston, Massachusetts, area.

He called me one day, and in the conversation, he said his mother was not doing well. She was a spry 95 years of age, and was still living on her own in the house she and my friend's dad built many years ago. The doctors did not know exactly what was going on, and sent her home with several new medications. She continued to get weaker and more ill, and my friend was growing concerned of how serious her situation was. He expressed that he had wanted to see his mother for quite some time, but the worry of catching a bug on commercial airline flights, and the risk of passing it along to her, had prevented him from traveling to see her in Boston.

I said to my friend: "Let's go." He hesitated and said what do you mean? I said: "Let's go see your mother. I will pick you up tomorrow morning in my airplane, and we'll fly to Boston to see her." He was thrilled and shocked at the same time, and quickly and enthusiastically agreed! We departed the next morning, and arrived in the Boston area in the late afternoon the following day. The flight went well, and we planned to stay about five days so he could help his mother get her medications straightened out and hopefully back on her feet. His arrival was a complete surprise, and I truly believe it restored her strength and willpower almost instantly.

During our stay, I gave my friend and his family as much privacy as I could. I spent a lot of time in their backyard, enjoying the nice fall weather that was cool and refreshing. I came to recognize and name the squirrels, rabbits, and each member of the neighborhood fox family. The mornings started with a run to Dunkin Donuts for a Box of Joe and other sweet delights. The best part is, his mother was quickly back on her feet and cooking up a storm in the kitchen! She is Sicilian, and I just happen to love Sicilian food!

But I am bored. To change things up early one afternoon, I decided to put on my sweatshirt, grab a cup of coffee, and go for a walk down the street. The neighborhood had nice homes that were built around the same time. My friend was raised in this neighborhood, and he said many of the homes were still owned by family members of those he grew up with. The layout of the streets in the suburbs were fashioned after wagon wheels from the early settler days. There was a center hub, with several streets spoking out in several directions. Each street / spoke was one block long with the house numbers running from 1 to 9. Then the next block, the street had a new name and the house numbers started all over again. Honestly, I don't think I could have gone more than a couple blocks without needing a GPS to get back!

The age of the neighborhood was apparent with the sidewalks bulging up from the roots of old, huge trees. Chain-link fences had short stubs of tree branches that had grown through and around the fencing over the years, and were simply cut off rather than destroy the fence. The streets were narrow with barely enough room for a car to pass down the middle with one parked on each side. Yet the neighborhood still proudly held generations of families and their memories and friendships, and they all continued to look after each other as they had done over the years.

After my walk, I returned to my friend's mother's house and went inside. A few minutes later, a police officer came to the front door. The officer asked if there was a stranger around here, saying he got a call that the neighbors saw a burglar walk into the house. My friend said yes, he is in the house, and the officer asked if he could have him step outside to identify him. My turn for a surprise. I walked outside, not knowing what was going on, and several neighbor ladies were standing in the middle of the street, pointing and yelling: "There he is! There he is! That's him!" I was shocked to see they were all pointing at me, for no reason at all. What did I do now?

My friend quickly explained we had just flown in together from Washington State to see his mother. The officer stood for a moment, looking at both of us, and never said a word to us or the neighbor ladies. He simply turned around, got in his squad car, and drove away. Picture me strolling down the street, about 1:30 pm on a cool, fall afternoon, carrying a cup of coffee, and wearing a sweatshirt that had an airplane on the back and my name stitched on the front! Needless to say, the neighbor ladies were very nice and apologetic to me for the rest of my stay.

I think back about that afternoon, as well as one of the historic places in the Boston area my friend had taken me to see. It was the Salem Witch Trials Memorial established in 1992. It memorializes victims who were executed during the witchcraft hysteria of 1692, where victims' lives were cut short by those who ignored their claims of innocence and the lack of proof. I can begin to understand how the collective hysteria of a few people, seeing something different and unknown, quickly escalates and is instantly assumed to be a danger. The victim is instantly guilty without a chance to be proven innocent.

After several wonderful days, seeing such great progress of my friend's mother's health, it was time to say our goodbyes and head west back to Washington. We departed the Boston area early in the morning, well before the sun came up. The weather was cloudy and rainy on our route, requiring me to fly on instrument flight plans in the poor to zero visibility. I did not have auto-pilot in the airplane, so I had to hand-fly the airplane the entire trip, which can be exhausting for even just an hour. By the time I arrived home, I had flown 17.1 hours, with the whole trip taking 18 hours and 45 minutes.

After dropping my friend off at his home town, I still had about an hour to go to our home and it was already well after dark. Diane had opened our hangar door, which was situated abeam the runway near the east end. She had also driven our golf cart out to the edge of the runway with the lights on to help me find the runway and line up for landing. I could not see the wind sock since it was dark, but quickly realized I had strong, horrific cross winds to deal with on landing, as well as a dark, unlit runway. I made a pass alongside the runway so I could set my landmarks and pinpoint the end of the runway. A quick circle and I was ready to land. I was exhausted and needed to be as sharp as possible, so I pulled from my years of experience, shook off the fatigue, and made a perfect landing. It wasn't until I was in front of our hangar that I realized just how hard the wind was blowing and gusting. I could feel the airplane rocking back and forth and even hear the wind once I shut the engine down.

All went well, and the trip was a great success. To see the look on that sweet 95-year-old lady's face when she saw her son made it all worthwhile. Another huge deposit in my bank of memories!

Chapter 25

OUR GUARDIAN ANGELS

We dedicated this book to our Guardian Angels. They have always been around us, and there are times we feel their presence. It is subtle, yet overwhelming, once one realizes the protective and loving arms you have embracing you. Our Angels are why we are here today to write these memoirs. Sanford and I both know we are still on this earth for a reason, although we are not quite sure why. As we stated in the beginning of this book – we know someday all will be explained to us.

In September of 2017 we took a week's vacation to go salmon fishing in the Strait of Juan de Fuca in Washington State with some good friends who knew all the good fishing spots. We had seen the pictures and heard the stories of how good the fishing was, so it was time to give it a try for ourselves. We had a 25-foot Bayliner boat that was capable of navigating these waters. It was small and cozy, and was equipped with a cabin that included all the amenities needed to live aboard for a week. We had done some weekend excursions, and we were anxious to take her out for an extended stay.

September weather is beautiful in the Pacific Northwest, and the crab season was open along with salmon fishing. We launched at Anacortes, Washington, and motored to one of our favorite destinations, Friday Harbor, Washington, in the San Juan Islands. We spent a couple of days there, crab fishing quite successfully, I might add, and picked a beautiful day to drive the boat across the Strait to Sekiu, Washington. We originally planned to go directly to Sekiu, but the morning we left Sanford decided to take a direct crossing and stop halfway in Port Angeles to get some fuel.

We were up before sunrise that morning to prepare the boat for the day-long trip. I was busy stowing our gear on the bow while Sanford was do his pre-flight, or pre-float, check of the engine and components. We had initially been in a hurry to get going, but the sense of urgency dissipated, and we took our time to make sure all was in order. The weather was beautiful, as we had anticipated, and the seas were nearly flat calm. It was a three-hour trip to Port Angeles, so we decided to take a break for lunch and walked into town for a bowl of clam chowder. The afternoon brought some showers and low clouds, and fog set in along the south shoreline of the Strait. We were equipped with new navigation equipment, including radar capable of detecting other boats and channel markers. We were driving the boat from inside the cabin and enjoyed being warm and comfortable.

It was about another three hours' travel from Port Angeles to Sekiu, and we arrived late in the afternoon at the marina in Clallam Bay.

Our friends had arrived that day as well, and already had their boats launched and tied up at the dock. Since we were going to stay aboard the boat for a few days, we were assigned a docking spot in another area of the marina, close to fresh water and the fish cleaning station, but no power hookup, and no cell service. We knew that before we arrived and came prepared with a portable generator since we needed lights, heat, and hot water. A few housekeeping items and we were set up for the night and focused on getting ready to go fishing early in the morning.

It was Monday morning and a cloudy day. The winds were light, and the ocean swells were smooth but building. We headed north across the Strait to our friends' favorite fishing spot. We had lots of bites and lost a lot of bait, and managed to bag our limit of nice-sized salmon. I had never fished for salmon in the ocean before, and it was a thrill to have one on the hook and land it in the boat!

The biggest thrill, though, was watching the whales! We were blessed with a continuous show of gray whales all around us for several hours that day. I lost count how many we had seen, but would estimate it to be near a hundred. Some close, and some far away that we could see blowing when they surfaced. The close whales were amazing, and we felt privileged to see them so nearby. There were two that seemed to follow us for a while, and then disappeared under the surface. A minute or so later, wow! One of the whales breached the water right alongside our boat for quite a show! We felt lucky to be on the water that day and experience such a gift of nature. It was mid-afternoon and we had been fishing all day, so we decided to head back to the marina.

Just as we returned it started to rain. Sanford still needed to clean the fish, just down the dock from where we parked the boat. I decided to straighten things up in the cabin of the boat and get the generator going to keep the freezer and fridge cold. We outfitted our boat with a small deep freeze on the back swim platform to keep the crab and fish frozen until we got home. It worked great since we were already using the generator to power the boat at the dock.

Now it is raining and the winds are completely calm, so a layer of fog seemed to be setting in along the shoreline. Sanford finished cleaning the fish, so we vacuum-packed them and added them to the freezer. Sanford is soaking wet and cold and ready for a nice, warm shower. And as soon as he was done, it was my turn.

We were trying to decide what to fix for supper since we hadn't eaten since breakfast, and our friends arrived that we had just been fishing with. We all sat down at the booth-table, making plans for where to fish the next day. It was early evening, we chatted for a while, apparently, and they left saying we looked tired from being in the fresh air all day and needed some sleep. Neither of us remember them leaving, but they said we were conscious and talking.

The following events are still foggy in both our memories.

What we do know is that sometime well after dark, Sanford woke up to find himself very confused on the floor of the boat. He saw me on the floor of the boat, having also passed out and falling the other direction, face down on the carpet. Sanford was unable to stand, with his head and chest hurting, so he crawled over to me and realized he was feeling sick and was going to throw up. He tried to wake me, with no response, and said I wasn't breathing. Sanford pushed open the door of the cabin and crawled out on the back deck of the boat to throw up over the side. Feeling that small burst of energy after being sick, he crawled back into the cabin to try and wake me again. Sanford collapsed and passed out again alongside me. He woke up, again, and realized we were in the fight for our lives. Sanford said at that moment in the boat he was not going anywhere without me, one way or the other.

For all our forty years of dating and married life, our time we spend together is precious. So much so that we always make it a priority to spend as much time together, especially when we were both working full time and were small business owners on the side. We worked hard, and we played hard, enjoying the satisfaction of both.

My first moment of consciousness in the boat was feeling like I was floating, face down, in the darkness with some sort of beings around me. It was not scary, actually quite peaceful, and I wondered where I was. Then I heard Sanford's voice above me. "Dear, come on dear, you need to get up. Come on Diane, you have to get up." I remember thinking, Sanford needs me, so I have to go. I have to get up, because he needs me. Then I am fully conscious and realize I am face down on the carpet, and cannot understand how I got there. Sanford is shaking me and still telling me I need to get up, but I can't move. I see my hands, but they don't work. I try to move my legs, but they don't work. Finally, I am able to get my hands under me and push up on my hands and knees with Sanford's help. And then I realize it feels like my head is going to explode, far worse than any migraine I have ever experienced. Both our ears are ringing and whooshing so badly we can hardly hear each other.

Sanford is still physically ill and soaking wet from being outside in the rain. I am amazed at his strength and wherewithal and determination. He was able to set the boat's dining table down that makes into a bed, and lift me onto it. He had to help me roll to the back so that he could lay down as well. Not having the strength for anything else, Sanford left the door of the cabin open, and our heater is running because the generator is still running. But we are both cold and shivering beyond control. We had blankets at our feet, but could not reach them. We had sleeping bags in the v-berth of the boat, an arm's length away, but could not reach them. All we had the power to do was lay there and fight to breathe.

Sanford kept asking me how I was feeling. My chest was hurting and my head would pound every time I tried to talk. Sanford knew we needed fresh air, and we both just wanted to sleep and hopefully feel better in the morning. We were both feeling sick now, but we were too weak to move. Eventually I was having trouble breathing. With the chest pain and tremendous headache, I wondered if I had a heart attack. He checked on me again, and I told Sanford I couldn't stand the pain in my chest any longer.

He found an unbelievable inner strength. He was determined to get us help. With no cell service, calling 9-1-1 was not an option. Sanford had to find someone to help us, and he kept saying we needed pure oxygen. He crawled out the boat and onto the dock that was wet and slippery from the rain. He crawled up the ramp from the dock to shore, and I could hear him throwing up all the way. Sanford found one of our friends sleeping in his van in the parking lot, and banged on the door, still on his hands and knees in the gravel. He told him we needed help and needed oxygen, and that he had to help get me out of the boat to shore. They wrapped me in a blanket and somehow got me off the boat…I don't remember much. After getting me into the van, Sanford actually fell inside the slider door of the van and was exhausted. Our friend had to pull Sanford's feet inside to be able to close the door.

None of us were from the area so we had no idea how to get to a hospital. We knew there was one in Port Angeles, but it was at least a two-hour drive, and Sanford knew we needed help before that. We decided to drive to where our other friend was staying nearby with his family, and ask what to do. On the way, Sanford was begging our friend to pull over because he was going to be sick again. Our friends knew we needed help fast. Clallam Bay is a very small town with a population of around 500 people. Just three months before, they received a federal grant and their volunteer fire department acquired an ambulance. It was parked just two blocks away.

Within a few minutes the ambulance arrived with three EMT's, and they helped both of us inside. They had one gurney and a bench on the side where they strapped me in sitting up. The ambulance was equipped with two oxygen masks and systems. They immediately put us both on 100% oxygen, and once secured, we headed to a town called Forks, Washington. After being on oxygen for a while, my headache backed off enough that I could think clearer, and my hearing improved. Sanford said he noticed after a few minutes, everything got very bright in the ambulance, and his hearing improved as well.

We spent the night in the emergency room, constantly on 100% oxygen. When we arrived, they moved us from the ambulance to the ER. Now off the oxygen, just for those few minutes, our symptoms quickly returned to a full roar. The nurses began fitting me with just the nose tube for oxygen rather than the face mask. I could hear Sanford hollering at them to give me a face mask, that we needed 100% oxygen. The nurses quickly changed me over to a mask, as another nurse was helping Sanford. They helped us fill out the necessary paperwork, and gave me a pen to sign. I couldn't remember how to write my name. We had a young doctor in the ER who was very skilled and attentive, who confirmed Sanford's conclusion of what happened to us in the boat.

Carbon monoxide poisoning.

We had spent many weekends on our Bayliner by that time, and had used our portable generator many times as well when we did not have access to shore power. We always placed it on the back deck, out in the open air, and always felt safe and secure knowing we had taken every precaution. That night at the dock in Clallam Bay, we did the same thing. But then, it started to rain. We draped the generator with a rubber mat to help protect it from the rain. It rained harder, so we placed a large plastic tub over the top to keep it dry. We felt it was a very important piece of equipment, especially for this trip, and we needed to protect it. The generator eventually melted a hole in the tub, and with the generator pushed to the side of the back deck, out of the way so we did not trip over it or the cords, the exhaust was pointing straight at a hole in the transom of the boat that was designed to hold fishing rods. The transom was wide open into the engine compartment, as well as the hollow side gunwales of the boat that held cables, wires, and hoses alongside the cabin. The exhaust filled the engine compartment and gunwales with carbon monoxide, and it seeped into the cabin. Our best guess, not remembering much from that night, is that we spent about seven hours breathing in that silent killer.

We learned a lot about carbon monoxide that night and over the next several months as we recovered. CO is odorless and colorless. It is nearly the same weight and density as the air, not heavier as we originally thought. CO will change weight and density with temperature and humidity, and can be at any level in the air. It can also accumulate just over the surface of open water on a calm, hot day. Soon after our accident, we heard a first-hand story of five boats tied together in a bay for an afternoon of swimming and grilling. The teenagers were swimming and enjoying the cool water, when one started having trouble staying afloat. They brought her to the back deck of one of the boats, where she was nearly unconscious. Then it happened to another teenager. They called the ambulance, and both were taken to the hospital with carbon monoxide poisoning. One of the boat's battery charger was not working, so he was idling his engine to get a full charge on the batteries. With no wind, the exhaust settled on the surface of the water immediately behind the boats, and the teenagers were quickly overcome with carbon monoxide.

Our ER doctor did a lot of research while we spent the night at the hospital. He kept questioning us about what happened, and we would re-tell the events as best we remembered. When we arrived at the hospital, they checked our blood oxygen levels, and we were at 86 and 87, with 99 to 100 being normal. Then they checked our CO saturation levels, and we were at 16 and 17, with zero being normal. Sanford somehow knew that night on the boat we needed something more than fresh air. We needed pure, 100% oxygen. The only treatment for CO poisoning is pure oxygen. It reduces the level of CO in the body by 50% every 90 minutes. Then you start the count again, reducing by 50% over the next 90 minutes. If you simply breathe, it would take your body 300 hours to expel the CO from your bloodstream, nearly two weeks. We calculated that we had been on oxygen about an hour by the time we arrived at the hospital when they checked our CO levels. When you run the numbers, that would mean Sanford and I were both at around a saturation level of 25.

We also learned that even though we are now able to function physically and mentally at our original capacity, permanent damage was done. We are extremely susceptible to any fumes and gases, but most especially to carbon monoxide and even our own carbon dioxide. Our lungs and bloodstream now absorb the chemicals at an extremely high rate, blocking oxygen from being absorbed in our systems. We take daily, natural supplements that help improve the nitric oxide in our systems and give us energy.

The reason the ER doctor kept questioning us is, in his words, they only see the saturation level of 25 in the morgue. Beyond that, not much is medically known about the long-term effects of such high concentration of CO. The doctor explained that there are less than 300 documented cases of survival, ever. The doctor also confirmed that you just don't wake up. Once you are unconscious, it is fatal unless someone finds you and is able to revive you.

Sanford woke up. Twice.

The morning we were preparing to leave Friday Harbor for our trip across the Strait of Juan de Fuca, we were both scurrying to get ready and be underway. I remember Sanford had slowed down and was methodically checking the entire boat and engine and components – exactly how he does before he flies an airplane. I learned right away when flying with Sanford, you can be in a hurry all you want, but when you get to the airplane, everything stops. Slowly and systematically the airplane is carefully pre-flighted for our journey. This is the same method Sanford always applies when we go boating, and this morning was even more so.

I did not know until we arrived home a few days later that Sanford experienced something that morning in Friday Harbor. He said he heard a voice say, clear as can be: "Be careful you don't die in Sekiu." Realizing no one was physically standing nearby to say it, he heeded the warning and took the time to be extra careful. Thinking we may have a problem with the boat, he checked every detail to make sure we were seaworthy. That's when he decided we would do a straight, shorter sea crossing to Port Angeles for fuel, and do another full check of the systems to ensure all was still good with the boat.

Then again, on that nearly-fatal night in the boat, while we were both laying there and fighting to breathe, Sanford heard the same voice: "You've got to get pure oxygen." I had just told him I couldn't stand the chest pain any longer, and with help, he found the strength to get up and get help. I remember him saying, as he left the boat for help: "We need pure oxygen. We have to get oxygen." I thought at the time, how did he know?

We were in the protective custody of our Guardian Angels.

The doctor said no one wakes up. Sanford did. Twice. He saved my life that night, again.

We are truly blessed to be here today, knowing God deemed us worthy of being two of his miracles.

God bless our Guardian Angels.

CPSIA information can be obtained
at www.ICGtesting.com
Printed in the USA
BVHW091433150322
631522BV00014B/985